WINDOWS
TO
GOD
A GUIDE TO CHRISTIAN FAITH

WINDOWS
TO
GOD
A GUIDE TO CHRISTIAN FAITH

GARY L. GRAFWALLNER

Primix Publishing
East Brunswick Office Evolution
1 Tower Center Boulevard, Ste 1510
East Brunswick, NJ 08816
www.primixpublishing.com
Phone: 1-800-538-5788

Published by Primix Publishing: 12/26/2024

ISBN: 979-8-89194-377-3(sc)
ISBN: 979-8-89194-378-0(hc)
ISBN: 979-8-89194-379-7(e)

Library of Congress Control Number: 2024924984

PRIMIX
PUBLISHING
THE WRITE CHOICE

Dedicated to those who know they are the people of God and those who would like to be, but who are not sure it's possible.

Table of Contents

PREFACE

I wish to express my appreciation to the many people who have helped and encouraged me to write this book. Their willingness to raise questions and struggle with the mystery of this God who calls us and eludes us has fanned my own faith when it tended to all but flicker out. I am grateful to my wife, Gail, who believes in me; three un-named saints who touched my life in a weekend workshop and commissioned me; and to John Brody who challenged me to finish with the following remark, "When God gives us an idea, if we fail to act upon it He gives it to someone else?' Linda Alvord typed the material with her characteristic competence and efficiency. Richard Londgren has provided invaluable assistance and comments in editing the entire manuscript and strengthening it. Paul Kusche helped with the development of the prints.

THE PURPOSE OF THIS BOOK

On a frosty winter morning, I was peddling my bike to work invigorated by the air and thinking how great it was to be alive. About three blocks from my office I was hit dead center by a car. The driver was late for work and hadn't waited for her windows to properly defrost. Her car was traveling about twenty miles per hour when she turned onto the street from her driveway. She applied the brakes just before the car struck me. The bike was totaled out. I escaped with torn clothes, cuts, bruises, and a rattled nervous system. The accident could have been prevented if the driver had taken the time to carefully scrape off her window.

God gives us different windows through which He lets us see signs of His activity and presence. We cannot see everything from any one window but we can see something. We need to scrape off these windows regularly. Some of them are less smudged than others. There are both large picture windows and smaller windows. Some are easily missed just because they are very ordinary looking. What is happening to us, and within us, determines whether we see anything or something new every time we look through these windows.

In any meaningful relationship between persons, there is always the mystery of uncovering different dimensions of the other person as well as ourselves. In our relationship with God, there will always be elements of surprise, discovery, and offense. Now we only see in part but God is knowable. Being human can be fun. I'm glad I can share both a bit of what God has shown me of Himself and the view others have pointed out to me through various windows we can look. I hope you'll share anything you find helpful in this book, colored by your own vision, with others.

The current emphasis on feelings, self-expression, and awareness of self and others in the Human Potential Movement and the Pentecostal Movement has been a needed corrective to the academic and intellectual approach to the Christian faith. An emphasis on "head religion" without dealing with our feelings can end up being theoretical, impersonal, and difficult to apply to daily living.

One that stresses "heart religion", or feelings and relationships, over responsible thought can be about as solid as the morning fog which burns off the noonday sun. Feeling God's presence is no substitute for a thoughtful faith. The Scriptures emphasize the importance of both.

I first began to look for God in earnest during my college days. At that time, I became rather skeptical about whether I could see or know anything concrete about Him. As I look back on those days my existence was like an empty house. Here and there were pieces of antiquated furniture but the rooms were drab apart from religious clutter in the corners. While preparing for a career in marine biology I became increasingly unsure about my purpose in life. It was during this occupational crisis that I began to ask some ultimate questions about the meaning of my existence.

I have since changed jobs. God has given me a new sense of direction and purpose. I am still asking questions about what we can see through various windows. In the following pages, I deal with some of the questions I have raised or heard people like yourselves ask as they grope for God in this topsy-turvy world. You may feel that you already see quite clearly through some of the chapter windows. Other chapters may give you a broader view, a heightened appreciation for a familiar scene, or a way to share a part of the picture with someone still struggling to find the "abundant life."

As you read ask God to speak to you through me and inspite of me. He has nudged me to indulge in this "foolishness." I have observed that for those who care to look a second time, or even a third, there are new sights to see.

I'D LIKE YOU TO MEET GOD

While dining out this past winter, my wife and I were approached by a young couple handing out tracts on the street corner as we entered a restaurant. They were collecting money for Bangladesh relief. I told them we had already given some money. They thanked us and gave us a tract even though we hadn't given them a donation. The tract contained portions of the Hindu Vedas, the oldest Scriptures of India.

While traveling on a train across the country this summer, a passenger pointed out a man who periodically arose each day and took a reed mat into the men's room. He said he accidentally walked in on the fellow and found him on his knees in prayer facing the East and Mecca. He worshipped Allah as a Muslim.

Recently two young men walked up the West Coast from Southern California to Seattle, Washington. One of them pulled a cart with all their gear. The other bowed and touched the ground every third step. They were on a mission of peace and were going to examine some property that had been donated to their monastery. One was a former Jew, the other a former Roman Catholic. They both had converted to Buddhism.

I'm increasingly uncomfortable when people tell me they believe in God. The word "god" can have a thousand different meanings for as many people. Who's "god" is really God?

Many Americans I talk to see God as outdated, a scapegoat, a genie in the sky, a benevolent softy, or an illusive phantom. I'm always interested in people's responses to the question, "Do you believe in God?" Often they reply, "Yes." The longer we talk the more apparent it becomes that for them God is often a nondescript carryover from childhood church school who makes no significant difference in daily living, self-understanding, or their relationships with others as an adult. Why believe in a god who makes no real difference?

A college sophomore walked into my office one afternoon and said, "I came to find out where you are with God." Where are you with God? I'm going to assume that you are somewhat interested. You may be very active within the Church or you may never have read a Bible. You may have drifted away from God but something or someone has begun to draw you back. You may have some vague sort of belief in a supreme being but have never taken the time to check out that belief.

For us to know God, we must be willing to let God be God instead of reducing Him to a manageable size. This involves a willingness to live with both the reality and the mystery of His presence. Whenever God discloses Himself to us He is also concealed. Anytime we learn something new about Him much remains hidden.

When we have a group of people in our home who don't know each other, now and then we play a game called The Five Senses. We ask each person to silently pick out their favorite smell, sight, taste, touch, and sound. Then we take each sense separately and ask them to share their choice.

The favorite smell might be baking bread or freshly mown hay, or the fragrance of lilacs. The favorite sight might be lightning flashes during an electrical storm, children playing uninhibitedly on monkey bars, or lovers holding hands. Favorite touch has turned up walking barefoot in the mud, sifting earth through your fingers, or petting a dog. For favorite taste, biting into a crisp apple, eating fresh corn on the cob with lots of salt and butter, or a glass of cold water on a hot day are choices that often surface. Favorite sounds have ranged from the soft coo of a morning dove, to popcorn bouncing off the inside of a kettle, to breakers crashing on the beach. Besides getting acquainted each of us comes away with a new appreciation for the world around us.

One window through which God discloses Himself is creation. There is a world outside our offices, homes, and factories. If we thoughtfully examine that world and reflect on its beauty, design, and the interdependency of its parts it is unreasonable to say all of this happened quite accidentally. The odds of that happening would be about as unlikely as throwing a Webster's unabridged dictionary into the air and having it come down all assembled and indexed in alphabetical order.

There is beauty, design, and balance between the parts of creation which suggests an intelligent purpose behind the world. It is visible in a community of ants colonizing a sidewalk crack, the beauty of Orion on a clear night, and the complexity with which the human brain responds to various stimuli. It is reflected in a flock of migrating Canadian geese, life in a hive of bees, or the reproductive process of the common night crawler. Surely all of this couldn't have just happened by coincidence. It fits together too well, as is becoming all too apparent in environmental studies. "Something must be behind it all," is the popular response I receive again and again when people start telling me why they believe God exists. If we open our eyes to the wonderful order of creation around us it does appear purposeful and therefore personal.

Archeologists and paleontologists continue to unearth primitive cultures which indicate some awareness of a power or being who is greater than humans. This being creates and sustains the creation. God is given many names which suggest part of the Divine nature we observe through this window. God might be called the Great Spirit, the Creator, the Almighty, our Maker. Through our created world we are given a glimpse of God's power and might. But this glimpse raises many questions. On the one hand, we have the beauty and interdependence of all living things, and on the other hand natural calamities such as earthquakes, tornadoes, and floods. What kind of a God is this Creator? He is in the words of one man, "an unknown God."

"That which you worship, then, even though you do not know it, is what I now proclaim to you. God who made the world and everything in it, is the Lord of heaven and earth and does not live in temples made by men. Nor does He need anything men can supply by working for Him, since it is He Himself who gives life and breath and everything else to all men. From one man He created all races of men and made them live over the whole earth. . . He did this so that they would look for Him, and perhaps find Him as they felt around for Him. Yet God is actually not far from any one of us; for 'In Him we live and move and are.'" (Acts 17:23-27 T.E.V.)

O God, there is evidence of your presence all around me. In the story of the rocks and the adaptability of plants and animals. But why is it so difficult to know you? If you created us, one would think that you wouldn't keep us guessing. Have you done all you can to let us know what you're really like, or are you so different from all that you've made that you are incomprehensible? Is there nothing with which we can compare you? Clear away my misconceptions. I want to know you personally. I would like to believe that's possible. Amen.

THE GOD COMPLEX

God has created the universe in such a way that everything is organized around a center. An atom has a nucleus around which protons, neutrons, and electrons travel. A cell has a nucleus that serves as a clearing house and control center. The movements of our body are directed by our brain. The moon moves around the earth; the earth rotates around the sun. Humankind was not created to be its own center but to know, honor, and serve the One who created all things. In other words, we were created to enjoy God and bring joy to God.

Imagine a group of children playing in a field. They see a dirt pile; perhaps the result of an excavation for a new building. They crawl, slide, and inch their way to the top. Then one decides that he should be the only one at the top. A game may ensue with the others challenging his boast. Eventually, the strongest holds the top of the pile and declares himself "King of the Mountain." He or she lords it over the others.

Each of us has, in our own way, pulled a big "rip off" on God. We have usurped the position that belongs to God alone and set ourselves up as counterfeit lords. We do not serve God; we serve ourselves. We would rather play God than obey God. We cannot plead ignorance or innocence. We have set ourselves up as "number one." God has given us the freedom to do as we please and we have damned ourselves by doing just that instead of pleasing god.

Some people call this rebellion "sin." The consequence is death or separation from God and each other. We no longer know who we are or whose we are. Our problem is not what we do but who we are. We are not what we could be. The deception in the national government, the exploitation of undeveloped countries, the skyjacking and kidnapping, the games being played with the price of oil and gasoline, the raw sewage or industrial waste dumped into our rivers and oceans, the violence in the streets, and greed that evokes another strike are symptomatic. They mirror the death in each of us. We breathe but do not live.

The novel *Lord of the Flys* is a story about a group of boys who are forced to set up their own society when their plane crashes on an island and all the adults traveling with them are killed. Before long the boys begin to assume different responsibilities and lay the ground rules for their society. On the basis of interest and ability, they naturally divide into the leaders and followers. The hunters are strong and aggressive and the thinkers are less physical and more passive.

Gradually, the novelty wears off. Sharp words are spoken and fights occur. The strong bully the weak. Scapegoats are sought and some of the boys become very vicious. Relationships deteriorate until the boys start hunting one another, first in sport and then in earnest. I felt like shouting, "What's wrong with them? Why don't they stop it?" The drama builds until only a few of the boys are left. Ironically, the survivors are rescued by a military destroyer. The world of the children is but a window through which we see the adult world. The difference being children are not always as sophisticated in concealing their true feelings or their instruments of destruction as adults are.

We have chosen to be like God, to "know good and evil." Each of us has somehow accepted the lie that the world should evolve around us and that we can make it on our own without

God. What began as fun has become a nightmare. In our effort to become self-sufficient, we have lost control. Like Adam in the biblical story of creation, we are afraid of God, threatened and at odds with one another, and we lack peace within. The name of the game has become survival and we are running scared.

"They know God, but they do not give Him the honor that belongs to Him. . . They say they are wise, but they are fools. . . Because humans refuse to keep in mind the true knowledge about God, they have given them over to corrupted minds so that they do the things they should not." (Romans 1:21, 22, 28 T.E.V.)

"All our righteous deeds have become like a polluted garment." (Isaiah 64:6 R.S.V.)

"I know that good does not live in me — that is, in my human nature. Even though the desire to do good is in me, I am not able to do it. I don't do the good I want to do; instead, I do the evil that I do not want to do." (Romans 7:18-19 T.E.V.)

God, are you still there, still listening? Something's wrong. I am wrong. It's not just my neighbor; it's me. It's as though we are trapped in a disaster of our own doing. We know what we do is wrong, but we do it anyway. Can you do anything to help? Amen.

HOW ODD OF GOD TO CHOOSE THE JEWS

In the play "Fiddler on the Roof" the leading male character, Tevye, a Russian Jew, sings a song, "Tradition." "Because of our tradition," he says, "every one of us knows who he is and what God expects him to do." As the plot develops, the words reoccur pointing to the tension someone who believes in God feels when he weighs his own experience of God with that of other people, be they his forebearers or own children. Tradition can be a blessing or a curse. We are partly a product of our past. Knowing our past can help us to understand ourselves today.

Another way this unknown God becomes more knowable to us is through the experiences, the ups and downs, of a people — a particular people. They were no better than any other people. As a matter of fact, their culture is fairly recent, dating back some three thousand years plus. God had to start somewhere. It could have as easily been near the Shanghai River as the Euphrates. But He communicated His presence to one man, an itinerant shepherd named Abram. God told Abram that through him and his descendants, the world would come to know God's love.

I remember one man asking, "Why did God pick such a nobody for such an important job?" He remarked, "If I were doing it, I'd have picked a king, or a president, or a world conqueror." As I suggested earlier, God often fails to meet our expectations. He frequently acts in ungodlike ways. God limited Godself and God's power when God said to Abram, "You and your descendants will be a light to the nations." So it was that Israel came to have a unique role as a window of God.

One of my good friends frequently says, "We're all heretics. Each of us distorts God in his own way." Israel was no different from you and me. She had a lot of misconceptions. Some of them were: That her God, Yahweh or Elohim, was just one god among many; that her god wanted child or animal (blood) sacrifice to offset peoples' sins (Abram); that her god was a law giver who clobbered those who refused to obey (Moses); that her god was a tribal deity who told her to sack enemy cities, utterly destroying the inhabitants and contents (Joshua); that her god could be housed in the temple (Solomon); or that her god was prejudiced in favor of Israelites (Jonah).

More than one person has said to me, "In the Old Testament God seems like a tyrant. God scares me." There certainly are pictures that reinforce this image. But they are not God speaking for God's self as much as humans trying to understand this strange God of many names who calls them to absolute obedience.

However, it is through Israel we also begin to learn that God is one and God has tremendous love for people. He is like a loving father who raises, guides and protects His helpless children. God is like a husband who passionately loves his wife and remains faithful to her even when she has other loves. God buys back the Jewish people when they have made a waste of their lives, salvaging them from the junk pile. This God saves the Hebrew people, liberating them from those things which restrict and dehumanize them. As far as the East is from the West, God removes their sins and drops the charges against them. Yahweh sobs and suffers when God's people ignore or reject Him to their own destruction. God's love tempers God's tremendous power. God's chief delight is that all people come to know Him. God asks we practice justice and kindness, loving our neighbors as ourselves.

It is through Israel then, that God begins to show Godself as not merely the unknown creator god, but the strong and tender one who is gracious and who will not abandon the people. He becomes involved in their history and hope, their prosperity and peace in warfare, and their grossness and greatness.

One book that has helped me to appreciate in a new way what God has done and disclosed through Israel is James Mitchner's historical novel, The Source. In it, he describes in a masterful way how the Jews are a unique witness, by their very survival, to the promise that God will preserve a remnant through His constant kindness and undeserved goodness. Israel's story is our story, for it is a window through which we all need to look to begin to understand who creates a community who are called to be His people and bear witness to Him.

Now therefore if you will truly obey my voice and keep my covenant, then you will be a particular treasure to me of all, for all the earth is mine. And you shall be for me a nation of priests, and a holy people. . ." (Exodus 19:5-6 .)

"And I will give you as a light to the nations, that my salvation shall reach to the end of the earth." (Isaiah 49:6 R.S.V.)

As a non-Jew, the Jews are a strange group of people to me, Lord. They're the brunt of many jokes and much prejudice. They are a divided house, from the militant Zionist, to the bearded conservative with his yarmulka, or the Kibbutzim dweller. They were given a high destiny by you, but like the rest of us their shallowness, lack of strength and long purpose, love of pleasure, comfort, and sloth has ended in tragedy. I need to learn more about their experiences with you. Many of them have forgotten they are "your planting." Yet, somehow I have the feeling that my heritage is related to theirs. If we are not brothers we may be cousins and the God of Abram could well be my God. Amen.

BEHOLD THE MAN

While attending summer school in Minneapolis, I saw a billboard with a black and white picture of Jesus similar to one popularized by the artist, Richard Hook. Beneath was the caption, "The Man With The Plan." This man is a picture window of God.

"No man ever spoke like this man," said His critics. "What kind of man is this that even the wind and seas obey Him?" asked His disciples following the stilling of a storm on Lake Galilee. And one author who met Him began his book by writing, "In the past, God spoke to our ancestors many times and in many ways through the prophets, but in these last days He has spoken to us through His Son."

But who is this smooth-skinned, Breck Shampoo Jesus whose picture is carried in so many wallets? Who is this Jesus who is painted black by a Tanzanian, almond-eyed by an Oriental, and a blue-eyed blonde by a Scandinavian artist? Who is this Jesus whose other-worldly gaze peers from a Greek Orthodox icon or who lies with eyes closed draped across Mary's marble lap in the Pieta? Who is this Jesus adorned in royal robes as Christus Rex above an altar in a Roman Catholic edifice? A pink reflector bumper sticker shouts, "Honk if you love Jesus" and in a prayer meeting people say over and over, "Thank you, Jesus. Oh, thank you, Jesus."

Jesus has many faces and that can be both helpful and confusing. It is easy to want to whittle Jesus down to our size, to accept what we can understand and dismiss or ignore that which bothers us. Is it any wonder that people have come away with a lopsided view of Jesus? Anyone seeking to learn of God in Jesus may be tempted to cry, "Will the real Jesus Christ please stand up!" I have been drawn to Jesus personally because of His own testimony, that of His followers, and the difference He made in their lives. The Good News of the Gospel declares the four following facts about Jesus: He is God; He was fully human; He died for our sins; and He was raised from the dead. This is what makes Him unique.

To say Jesus is God is not to say Jesus is all that God is, but that Jesus is fully divine. Jesus existed before He was born on earth. He was there in the beginning as the Creator. All things were made through Him and without Him, nothing was made that is made. He was involved in the creation of the atom and the atom splitter, man.

Someone once told me a story of a father sitting on the back porch with his son watching some ants. The boy asked his father if the ants knew he was there. The father replied, "I don't know." So, the boy got down on his hands and tried talking with the ants. They scattered and the son commented that the ants appeared afraid of him. He then made a path in the dirt from the small, granulated mound to the back porch of his home. A few scout ants checked out the path but the rest of the ant community continued, apparently oblivious of his presence. To show them he was friendly the boy went and got some bread, dipped small pieces in honey, and placed it in the path he made. When the word got around, the ant colony mobilized in mass to capitalize on this bonanza. The son was distressed because the ants accepted his gifts but still did not communicate with him. In reflecting on the situation, he turned and said to his father, "The only way those ants will know what I'm really like and that I don't intend them any harm is if I become an ant."

The Gospel announces that God did not become an ant but a human being. In Jesus God shows us something new about His love. He became one of us in this Jewish child, born of Mary. He grew up in a carpenter's shop and at an early age was very familiar with the smell of freshly cut wood. He was a student of the Torah and the Prophets. As He matured physically, he gradually became aware of His identity and mission as the Jewish Messiah. Like other men, however, He experienced fatigue, anger, grief, temptation, and hunger. He was rejected by friends, misunderstood by His family, and knew the panic of facing His own death alone. He did not play favorites and could love equally a member of the upper class like Nicodemus, a commercial fisherman like Peter, and a Roman soldier who represented the occupation troops in His native country. He exposed the religious games people play and offered healing, forgiveness, and new life to all who would admit they were not whole people. He said, "I and the Father are one. If you believe my words, you believe the One who sent me." And when people grew angry with His claims of divinity He asked, "Which of you convicts me of sin? You search the Scriptures because you think that in them you have eternal life, and they bear witness to me. Yet you refuse to come to me that you might have life."

In Jesus, we see the kind of person God wills each of us to be. The problem is we just aren't there. There is no way we can be perfect, and perfection is what God demands. "You shall love me with all your heart, soul, mind, and strength and your neighbor as yourself." Because we chose not to, we live under His judgment. We are disoriented, self-centered, uptight, fearful, greedy, and overindulgent sensualists. In playing god we lose touch with God and ourselves. The symptoms of death are visible at drive-in theaters and in the contemporary novel, the city jails and the rest homes, the number of single young girls and women who pop a pill to avoid pregnancy and the growing divorce rate, the percent of heart attacks in young men and the increase in alcoholism, the accidents caused by speeding and the pilfering at the plant. There is no way we as humans can undo the damage, bridge the gap, or earn enough brownie points to come back into fellowship with God. We are at war with God. The wages of sin are death. But the free gift of God is eternal life to all who believe in the sinless one.

A friend of mine witnessed an automobile accident on his property. Two brothers were out for a ride in a new car. The father had given it to the elder brother. The youngest wanted to drive but his brother refused because he didn't have a license, he was too young, and the father had said he couldn't handle the car due to its powerful engine. They stopped in town at a store. When the older brother came out of the store the younger brother refused to move from behind the steering wheel even after much pleading and warning. On the way home the younger brother lost control and totaled out the car. He went to pieces. Sobbing, he said over and over, "Why didn't I listen to father. He told me I couldn't handle it. How can I face him? What can I say?" My friend who had called an ambulance and notified the police was standing within earshot when he saw the older brother crawl out of the back window, climb up the side of the car, enter the window on the driver's side, and push his brother to the other side of the front seat. He sat down and said, "Be quiet. I'll take the blame."

And he did. God loves us so much that even though we don't deserve to come into His presence He lets His Son take the blame for our sins. That forgiveness isn't cheap; it's costly. God Himself pays the price for our disobedience. That's the reason I want to say, "Thanks" with my lips and my life.

"Surely He has born our griefs and carried our sorrows. . . He was wounded for our transgressions and bruised for our iniquities; upon Him was the chastisement that made us whole, and with His stripes we are healed. All we like sheep have gone astray; we have turned everyone to his own way, and the Lord has laid on him the iniquity of us all." (Isaiah 53:4-6 R.S.V.)

"The next day John saw Jesus coming toward him and he said, 'Here is the Lamb of God who takes away the sins of the world.'" (John 1:29 T.E.V.)

"He was teaching His disciples, saying to them, 'The Son of Man will be handed over to men who will kill Him; three days later, however, He will rise to life.' But they did not understand what this teaching meant and they were afraid to ask Him." (Mark 9:30-32 T.E.V.)

"We have a great high priest who has gone into the very presence of God — Jesus. . .who was tempted in every way we are but who did not sin." (Hebrews 4:14-15 T.E.V.)

"God puts men right through their faith in Jesus Christ. . .all men have sinned and are far away from God's saving presence. God offers Jesus so that by means of His death He should become the means by which men's sins are forgiven through their faith in Him." (Romans 3:22-23, 25 T.E.V.)

Lord, thank you for becoming one of us. You seem more real and less remote in Jesus. Thank you for dying so we might live. Amen.

YOU CAN'T KEEP A GOOD GOD DOWN

Anyone who speaks the truth is a threat to someone who lives a lie. Those who champion God's cause become vulnerable to innuendo, telephone threats, the possible loss of their job, citizenship, or life. Darkness cannot stand the light. For Solzhenitsyn the opposition used banishment. For Medgar Evers, Martin Luther King, two of the Kennedy brothers, the enemy used a bullet. For Jesus it was death by nails and suffocation on a cross.

His enemies must have breathed a sigh of relief that this Jewish meddler was out of the way once and for all. Business could continue as usual in Pilate's palace, the Temple, and the streets of Jerusalem. He was long gone, or so they thought, sealed in a tomb No one had returned from the grave. His followers had scattered for fear the heat might be turned on them. The ripple caused by His life in the pond we call Israel was fast fading.

Jesus would have been remembered as a good man who had high ideals and who cared for people regardless of their education, economics or ethnicity, save for one thing. They couldn't silence Him. They tried their best. They killed Him but God the Father raised Him. And the rumor spread. The unbelievable began to be believed. "He is not dead but alive. You will see Him." And they did. Not everyone in the larger circle of disciples was convinced. Unbelief dies hard. Some thought it was wishful thinking. Others saw it as a swift political move to create a myth of a risen hero and perpetuate the Nazarene's sect. But no mere story transformed cowards into the greatest revolutionaries the world has ever seen. Only one person, Jesus Himself, could have convinced them it wasn't all over for them or Him. He appeared and reappeared in a garden, on a beach, behind locked doors, on a mountain top: to women, fishermen, a skeptic, to individuals and crowds again and again.

God vindicated His Son. He used the cross as a battering ram to knock the ends out of every casket and let in the light of eternal life. Jesus was not a phony, a con artist, or mentally ill. His claim to exist before Abraham is not false. While He no longer walks among us in human flesh, He is alive and well. This God whose creation had no room for Him, reigns over our world and all worlds as the exalted Lord.

The news is as much a surprise and offense today as it was when whispered for the first time by those who thought their eyes or minds were playing tricks on them. I don't understand the Resurrection, but I celebrate it. As a child I was told about Jesus but somewhere along the line I never quite understood the truth that He is knowable today. I tried to read the Bible but it always seemed so other worldly. Whenever people spoke to me about Him it was always in the past tense. "Jesus did this. Jesus said that." I don't remember hearing people speak about their experiences with Him in the present tense.

Perhaps you know Jesus only as a historical figure. You may know about Him — the story of His birth, ministry, death, resurrection, but not know Him personally. To know He is the Saviour of the world and supreme Lord over all the universe is greater than having Him as your personal Saviour and Lord.

I began to know Him as a real living person through a biography of Peter Marshall, a Presbyterian pastor. It was given to me at a time when I was searching. I am amazed how Jesus discloses Himself to each person in a way that permits them to begin to know Him. After reading this book I felt if Jesus could be that real for the author, then I wanted to know Him too. Since my university days our relationship has matured to the point where He is the most important person in my life. It didn't happen overnight. There have been a lot of ups and downs. I still have questions and much to learn. He is worth knowing and knowable.

He wants you to know Him and experience His life and power, too. I believe it was Sam Shoemaker, an Episcopalian rector, who once said, "If you give as much of yourself as you can to as much of Jesus Christ as you can understand, you will grow." Easter announces "You can't keep a good man down, especially if that man is God Himself. He has come that you might have life. Interested?

"I passed on to you what I received, which is of greatest importance; that Christ died for our sins, as is written in the Scriptures, that He was buried and raised to life on the third day. . .that He appeared to Peter, then to all twelve apostles. Then He appeared to more than five hundred of His followers at once. . .Then He appeared to James, and then all the apostles. Last of all He appeared to me. . ." (1 Corinthians 15:3-8 T.E.V.)

"Let us give thanks to the God and Father of our Lord Jesus Christ! Because of His great mercy He gave us new life by raising Jesus from the dead. This fills us with living hope. . ." (I Peter 1:3 T.E.V.)

"God made the world through Him, but the world did not know Him. He came to His own country, but His own people did not receive Him. Some, however, did receive Him and believe in Him. So, He gave them the right to become God's children. They did not become God's children by natural means by being born as children of a human father, God himself was their Father." (1 John 1:10-13 T.E.V.)

Jesus, thank you for appearing to me now and then. Thank you for appearing to others who remind me you are alive when I forget. Thank you for the gift of faith which enables me to believe you are, and that you are here for us. I couldn't convince myself of this truth by myself; who you are and what you have done boggles my mind. Thank you for your life. Amen.

GOD IN THE PRESENT TENSE

"If I had only lived when Jesus did it would have been so much easier to believe." Have you ever made a statement similar to the one above? It sounds logical enough. Your experience could have been first hand. You would have seen Him in person, listened to Him teach, watched Him heal, asked Him questions face to face. Many people did exactly that and they were either angered or filled with admiration for Jesus of Nazareth, but the vast majority did not believe.

Jesus turned people off, partly because He didn't meet their expectations for God. Partly because faith does not depend on eyesight as much as inner sight or a willingness to let God disclose Himself as He chooses. One man wrote that "God in His wisdom has made it impossible for men to know Him strictly by means of their own wisdom." Jesus Himself said, "No one can come to me unless the Father who sent me draws Him." This does not refute all human knowledge as much as expose its limitations. We are incapable of believing in Jesus or coming to Him on our own.

God is no longer with us in the flesh. I'm not sure it makes much difference since I suspect most of us would have just as difficult a time believing today if someone from our neighborhood or a stranger we met at the supermarket or a friend of a friend claimed to be God. We'd probably chuckle, avoid this person, or assume the individual was emotionally upset or delusional. The first disciples of Jesus did not have any significant advantages over us. They knew even less about themselves and the earth. I'm convinced we can have a firsthand experience with God today that is just as personal, meaningful, and powerful. The question is how?

Jesus said, "I am going away. . .but the Counselor, the Holy Spirit whom the Father will send in my name, will teach you everything and make you remember all that I have told you. He will lead you into all the truth." In other words, the Holy Spirit is Jesus' replacement. He is the name we give to God's presence in us and among us today. He is "God with us" right now. He enables us to believe. None of us can say "Jesus is our Lord" and begin to grasp the implications of this statement without the Holy Spirit convincing us we are not engaged in self deception. The Holy Spirit introduces us to Jesus. He also explains the true significance of the work God began and will bring to completion in Jesus the Christ. He makes Jesus believable. If you have ever bought a house or business, you have probably made a down payment. The down payment was a sign you were serious about purchasing the house or property. You intended to follow through. God loves us. To show us He means business He comes to us and will actually give us Himself or the Holy Spirit as a down payment or first installment. In this way He demonstrates His desire to claim us as His very own people. One of the early Christians said, "This is how we are sure we live in God and He lives in us: He has given us His Holy Spirit." There is no way that I can personally convince myself of this on my own. I'm just too skeptical.

I remember worshipping in a suburban congregation on a particular Sunday when the subject of the sermon was "The Holy Spirit: His Nature and Work." The pastor spoke of the Holy Spirit as an "it," "he," "a force," "a power," "a thing." I wrote him a note, in love, during the offertory indicating that if his people were not thoroughly confused by he time he had finished preaching then the Holy Spirit must be working overtime.

The Spirit is not a force or a power but a personal and a purposive Being, who relates tc us in a meaningful and responsible way. He is God in the present tense. His coming may be marked by a quiet whisper or an overpowering presence that brings us to our knees. He calls us to Jesus, enters our bodies, incorporates us into the Body which we call the Church, and enables us to live for the Lord by letting Him live in us. He helps us overcome the self destructive elements within our personalities, teaches us how to pray, frees us up to be concerned enough to offer our lives in the service of others, even as our Lord stooped to wash His followers' feet.

"Would any one of you fathers give his son a snake when he asks for a fish? Or would you give him a scorpion when he asks for an egg? As bad as you are, you know how to give good things to your children. How much more then, the Father in heaven will give the Holy Spirit to those who ask Him!" (Luke 11:11-13 T.E.V.)

"To have your mind controlled by what human nature wants will result in death; to have your mind controlled by what the Spirit wants will result in life and peace. Whoever does not have the Spirit of Christ does not belong to Him. But if Christ lives in you, although your body is dead because of sin, yet the Spirit is life for you because you have been put right with God.

"If the Spirit of God who raised Jesus from death, lives in you, then He who raised Christ from death will also give life to your mortal bodies." (Romans 8:6, 9-11 T.E.V.)

O Holy Spirit, thank you for reassuring me I can have a dynamic relationship with God today. Sometimes I forget and start doubting. I wonder when I believe whether I am deceiving myself or have been duped by well meaning people. Teach me what I need to know about the nature of God's activity in Jesus and then empower me to be an effective follower of Jesus today. Amen.

DO YOU HAVE TWO BIRTHDAYS?

Late one October afternoon I was lying in bed enjoying the peace and quiet. I had been feeling rather dragged out and had a bad case of the "aches and chills." I happened to be reading. The rest of my family was gone with the exception of our oldest son who was nearly six at the time. He bounced onto the bed and began asking questions and chattered in what seemed an endless stream of words. At first I was annoyed. Realizing I had been gone a lot I decided to listen. He was all excited about his approaching birthday. He managed to get me out of bed to show me a pile of multicolor wrapped packages on the top shelf of a hall closet. He just couldn't wait to open them.

I snuggled back under the covers after our little excursion. It was then I asked him this question: "Do you know you have two birthdays?" He looked at me in disbelief and said, "You're kidding." I said, "No." He thought a minute and then said, "Do you mean I came home with you and mom from the hospital twice?" "No," I replied. "You were only born to us once. You were also born again as a result of God's love when you were baptized." He wanted to know if he'd gotten any presents for his second birthday. I told him he had received some but God had many others still to be opened.

Out of all the windows we have looked through together so far, this next one is probably one of the most smudged.

There has and will continue to be some strong differences of opinion over baptism by sincere and responsible Christians within the household of faith. Sooner or later the thoughtful believer must deal with baptism in a responsible way. Maybe you have wrestled with some of the following questions: "Are Spirit baptism and water baptism the same?" "Why baptize infants when they aren't conscious of what's happening? Wouldn't it be better to wait until they could experience the joy of this moment?" "If I have accepted Christ by faith and given Him permission to live in me, why should I be baptized?" "If baptism is a requirement for salvation are persons who never have an opportunity to be baptized lost?"

Part of the confusion over baptism is due to the fact that the New Testament witnesses are not consistent in what they say about baptism and how the Lord uses it. There is no one single incident or passage that gives us a complete picture of the meaning of baptism in the early Church. In the early Church, baptism is a water/Spirit baptism and a one time event. It is very easy to stress some passages and ignore others, but this is not a proper use of scripture. If we are to be honest we can't pick and choose but we need to live with the total biblical witnesses and that leaves some loose ends. Far too many believers I know end up riding a denominational hobby horse when it comes to the meaning of baptism.

The New Testament speaks again and again of baptism as God's act. It is not our acceptance of God but God's acceptance of us for Jesus sake. It is not a church ritual but the gift of God's Spirit to us. Jesus commanded that "all be baptized" in Matthew's and Mark's Gospel. In John's Gospel, Jesus is spoken of as the one who will baptize with the Holy Spirit. Luke refers to Him instructing the disciples to wait until they are filled with power when the Holy Spirit comes upon them. Baptism involves God doing something for us and with us that changes both our relationship with Him and our reason for being. It is a sign of new birth or beginning with God. Jesus said we must be born again of God's action.

Wherever baptism is mentioned explicitly or implicitly the Word and the Spirit are always spoken of in close proximity. The Word is the announcement of the good news of God's acceptance of us because of Jesus' sacrifice and resurrection on our behalf. The Spirit conveys this new life to us, as the go-between God. He enables us to hear and perceive this Word, turn and yield to Him, enter the Father's family, and be empowered as servant witnesses. That sounds wordy, but it's what I want to say.

In the New Testament, the Holy Spirit doesn't always come in the same way nor disclose Her presence uniformly. She can come like the wind, sometimes gently and other times dramatically. Sometimes it is quite evident she has already begun to work in a person's life, especially in an adult prior to their baptism. People were baptized in "the Name of Jesus," in "the Name of the Father, Son and Holy Spirit." There was the laying on of hands and prayers for the in-filling of the Holy Spirit. Persons respond to their baptism in the biblical accounts in such ways as: seeking and fellowshipping with other believers, using their gifts to strengthen the church, a new confidence in telling others of Jesus sacrificial service, by speaking in tongues, and through joy. The response varies from person to person.

Have you ever gotten an ink stamp on the hand when you went swimming, dancing, or skating? The ink stamp signifies someone has paid for your admission and you can come and go freely. In baptism, the apostle Paul says that the Holy Spirit stamps or brands us by letting us in personally on Jesus crucifixion and resurrection for our sakes. We can't go back to 29 A.D. but what He did once, for all people, becomes effective for you and me at our baptism. We are forgiven and accepted. In our baptism into Christ "we share in His death, so just as Christ was raised from death. . .we might live a new life." Baptism marks the death of living for oneself and the birth of being open to the new life of Jesus' Spirit in us. For both a child and an adult this new life and relationship must be nurtured. Baptism is not a heavenly insurance policy. One does not automatically grow with God. That would make baptism magic. We need the teaching and encouragement of other Christians to grow as God's person.

To be baptized involves being given a new name, a new family, and a new responsibility. God has only one natural Son, Jesus. The rest of us become His sons and daughters through adoption. In baptism we are given a new name, "child of God." We are received into His family. "the one holy, catholic, apostolic church," and not a particular denomination. We are all baptized into the same family of God by the Spirit. It is incorrect to say, "I was baptized Methodist, or Lutheran, or Roman Catholic, or Baptist." God baptizes us "into Christ." He incorporates us into Christ's Body, the Church. Anyone who is baptized receives tens of thousands of new brothers and sisters among whom our Father desires there be filial love. We are called to show concern for all people, but our relationship with every believer is unique by virtue of what Jesus has done for both of us. Henceforth, wherever we go we are a child of God among many brothers and sisters. Whether or not we desire to live as children who honor our Father is both the privilege and burden of being a believer. Many baptized persons are not living up to the implications of their baptism but this doesn't nullify God's act. It ignores it.

Two of our children are adopted. When we first learned of Jung Hee Jung and Shin Hae Jung we could have merely assumed financial support by regularly sending a check to cover their education, medical, and bodily needs. As they grew older they would become aware of the Grafwallner family who loved them. When they reached the legal age for adulthood they could have chosen whether or not to come and live with us. But we acted before they knew of our love. We wanted them to grow up living in an intimate relationship with us, so that each of us could experience the joys and sorrows, the victories and defeats, and share the others' love. So we had them flown to America; we paid the adoption fees. Now they bear our family name. Everything that is ours are theirs. It's great for them and for us.

God wants every person, regardless of age, to become His child. His love precedes ours. He can work apart from baptism but wills to use this means to bring us into a new relationship with Himself and His family. He does not violate our freedom for we can leave home any time we desire. For me, the entire Christian life has become living up to the implications of my baptism — exploring my sonship and continually asking how I am honoring my Father.

"'What shall we do, brothers?' Peter said to them: 'Turn away from your sins, each one of you, and be baptized in the name of Jesus Christ, so that your sins will be forgiven and you will receive God's gift the Holy Spirit. For God's promise was made to you and your children, and to all who are far away — all whom the Lord our God calls to Himself.'" (Acts 2:37-39 T.E.V.)

"Truly, I say to you, unless you are born of water and the Holy Spirit they cannot enter the Kingdom of God. That which is born of the flesh is flesh and that which is born of the Spirit is spirit." (John 3:5-6 R.S.V.)

"'Believe in the Lord Jesus,' they said, 'and you will be saved —you and your family.' And they preached the word of the Lord to him and to all the others in his house. At that very hour of the night the jailer took them and washed off their wounds, and he and all his family were baptized at once." (Acts 16:31-33 T.E.V.)

"Baptism saves you not by the washing off of bodily dirt but by the promise made to God through a good conscience. Baptism saves you through the resurrection of Jesus Christ." (1 Peter 3:21 T.E.V.)

"So Ananias went, entered the house and placed his hands on Saul. 'Brother Saul,' he said, 'the Lord has sent me — Jesus Himself whom you saw on the road as you were coming here. He sent me so that you might see and be filled with the Holy Spirit.' At once something like fish scales fell from Saul's eyes and he was able to see again. He stood up and was baptized. . ." (Acts 9:17-18 T.E.V.)

Father, I do not understand baptism, but you have said it is a concrete sign of your acceptance of me. I need that kind of reassurance. It is a wonderful mystery that marks the beginning of a new relationship with you and a new birth for me. In some ways it is like an engagement ring, a gift indicative of your love for me, a prelude to a more intimate relationship. Help me to daily cultivate my relationship with you and your family so that I will be ready for the wedding when Jesus comes to claim His bride, the Church. Amen

CLEARING THE AIR

The air was charged with electricity. A group of us had been challenging our professor in systematic theology on the meaning of confessing our sins and absolution. As the bell rang for the conclusion of the class hour he said with emphatic finality, "If you don't believe this you have no business being ordained. I hope you have guts enough to be honest." Some of us remained after class to continue the debate.

The issue was that each person is not his own priest. We cannot absolve ourselves. Each of us needs a priest. I led the rest of my senior class in pressing the point that there is only one mediator between God and mankind and that is Jesus. There is no need to go to a man when we can confess to God the Father directly through Jesus. Besides, we argued, what gives any man the right to do this since we have all sinned? Behind it all was human pride. Our professor pointed out that while only God has the power to forgive sin, He has given to the Church the authority to declare His forgiveness or the lack of it when someone remains unrepentant. He concluded by saying every Christian has the responsibility for this ministry of bearing the sins of other individuals and declaring God's forgiveness to them one to one, just as a pastor has it for a congregation. Even with all his historical and biblical documentation we were hardly convinced. Experience has changed this.

A middle age man I know became involved with his secretary. He thought she could meet all his needs. He divorced his wife of twenty years and married a woman half her age. Nine months later he realized his foolishness. He told this young woman he acted impulsively. His wife, who is a marvelous person, accepted him back. They were quietly remarried.

Four years have passed but he has never apologized to his teenage children nor asked their forgiveness. Their resentment smolders. Periodically it errupts. He is irritable, uptight, defensive, and can't wait for his kids to graduate from high school and move out. He drives himself in his job and his conversation is laced with negative remarks about the hypocrisy of others. His wife said to me, "He is so restless. It's affecting his health. If only he'd tell them he was sorry I believe he'd have peace." The last time I saw him he had bags under his eyes, he was chain smoking three packs a day, and he was talking about escaping from it all by retiring and developing some lake property he had purchased.

This is just one incident among many that have made me begin to realize how important it is for us to confess our sins to one another. Much of the information we are currently receiving from psychologists, psychiatrists, and students of human behavior indicates there is a very strong connection between mental and physical health and forgiveness. A friend of mine, a high school clinical psychologist, speaking to a group of parents said that one of the ingredients essential for being a healthy person is having a confessor.

I'm increasingly convinced that one of the most neglected areas of the church's ministry is hearing one another's confession. There are so many guilt ridden people walking around carrying the millstone of past misdeeds. They end up being emotional and sometimes physical cripples unable to experience the present possibilities of God's new life today because of it.

I hear a lot of private confessions and I encourage them because I've seen the release and relief that can come by lancing the abcess, but today we speak of it as pastoral counseling. This is not just my ministry but the ministry of every believer. There are people who may not be able to speak to anyone, including their pastor, but they could speak to you. We grieve the Holy Spirit when we back away from this ministry of healing. True, there are some individuals who need professional help. Many persons could be helped by friends who care and listen in love.

One of our denominational regional meetings was held in Boise, Idaho. Enroute four of us stopped at a little cafe for lunch. It was quite busy and we sat down at a table that had not been cleared off from the previous diners. The waitress snapped, "Don't sit at that table. It's dirty." We assured her we didn't mind but her anger was quite visible as she took our order and served us our meal. Each of us tried to be polite and gracious but she remained sullen. "It's okay; don't be so uptight," was something we all tried to communicate to her nonverbally. Unknown to one another, each of us prayed for the waitress. On our return trip we stopped at the same cafe, only this time we sat at a clean table. We wondered if the same waitress was still there. She was. She came to our table and with a smile said, "Today I'm having a better day." She was responding to the verbal and nonverbal absolution we had spoken to her several days earlier. Our forgiveness had made a difference.

The invisible God does not work in a vacuum. He becomes visible in His people. He will provide you with one or more persons with whom you can acknowledge those specific ways you have hurt Him and other people. He forgives specific sins and it's a wonderful experience to hear Him say through someone sitting across from you or standing next to you, "It's okay. I forgive you. You may start over again."

Dietrich Bonhoeffer said unwillingness to confess our sins to our brother simply affirms we are proud and have not really confessed our sins to God. You may say, "I just can't do it. That's too strong for me." Maybe this is one of the deeper mysteries of the Christian life, a truth too hard to swallow for someone who is spiritually an infant. All I know is many people have tried it and it works. We need forgiveness daily. But we also need the concrete, in the flesh reassurance that it's for real. The Church has lost sight of this truth and it's taken contemporary medicine and psychotherapy to remind us of its importance. We are called to bear one another's burdens. Only when we know we are accepted can we accept others.

"If we say we have no sin we deceive ourselves and there is no truth in us. But if we confess our sins to God, we can trust Him, for He does what is right. He will forgive our sins and make us clean from all our wrong doings." (1 John 1:8-9 T.E.V.)

"Then Jesus said to them, 'Peace be with you. As the Father has sent me so I send you.' He said this, and then He breathed on them and said, 'Receive the Holy Spirit. If you forgive men's sins they are forgiven; if you do not forgive them they are not forgiven.'" (John 20:21-23 T.E.V.)

"Therefore, confess your sins to one another and pray for one another so that you will be healed." (James 5:16 T.E.V.)

Our Father, thank you for other people who know me as I am and who can still forgive me. When someone wants to "come clean" with me, help me to hear their confession and not cut them off by saying or implying what they have done or neglected to do isn't all that serious. The pus must come out before the wound can heal. Then permit me as one who has also sinned and opposed your will to assure them that we don't have to be enslaved to our past. We can live again as free persons who walk upright like an exclamation point instead of curled in upon ourselves like a question mark. Amen.

THE ONLY UNFORGIVEABLE SIN

Have you ever wondered whether there is any sin God can't forgive? Like selling out a friend or business partner, letting your tongue run away from you and verbally committing murder, disgracing your parents, initiating or precipitating a divorce, playing fast and loose with someone else's body or not controlling your own, harboring an old resentment that smolders like a peat bog fire.

A church leader I know still blames himself because he feels at least partly responsible for his sister's suicide. Occasionally, someone may ask me "How can God continue to forgive a sin if I keep doing it over and over again?" It may involve profanity, adultery, losing our temper. Well, what do you think? Does He? Does there come a time when He says to us, "That's it. I've had it. You've pushed me too far. You have taken advantage of me too long. No more apologies, you phony." And the door slams in our face.

Jesus spoke in the Gospels of only one sin that was unforgiveable. He referred to it as the sin against the Holy Spirit. The context within which He spoke of this points to a person being closed to God's presence. Jesus suggests that you may deny or betray Him and still be forgiven, but if you harden your heart repeatedly to the Holy Spirit's efforts to draw you to Himself you may become incapable of responding. Thus, if you say "no" to the Spirit long enough you eventually won't or can't hear Him.

Like barnacles that grow upon barnacles, we can produce one layer after another of material that insulates us from God's love to the point where we are incapable of hearing, feeling, or responding to His call. It's frightening to think He gives us that kind of freedom.

A junior high student asked a colleague of mine if there were any warning signals a person could be alert to if he was in danger of committing this sin. My colleague replied, "Anyone who commits this sin wouldn't worry about the possibility of their committing it. As long as you feel the slightest twinge of guilt or remorse when you rebel against God and your neighbor there is hope." I would want to be quick to add none of us is in a position to judge whether another person is guilty of this sin. Some of the most an unlikely looking candidates for the Kingdom of God to our human eyes have done a flip flop and become outstanding heroes faith.

There are not degrees of sin or a hierarchy of sins. Jesus rejects this in the Sermon on the Mount (Matthew 5:21-30). Distinctions that make some behaviour more repugnant than others are man's doing, not God's. Sin is anything that gets between me and God, or me and my neighbor, or me and my trueself —what I'm capable of becoming under God.

Jesus came to our planet to save us from our sins. He is as capable of forgiving genocide or child abuse as he is religious prejudice or the parent who gives their children everything except themselves. Sodomy or rape is no more serious than going to bed with a partner whom you do not love. Litter in a campground or beer cans dropped under bleachers at a football game violates His creation as much as the air pollution caused by insisting we be a two car family or the energy drain caused by the electric dishwasher, rotisserie, and the like. The only unforgiveable sin is not wanting to be forgiven. Everything else God can handle.

As far as the east is from the west, so far does He remove our transgressions from us." (Psalm 103:12 R.S.V.)

"God has now brought you to life with Christ; God forgave us all our sins. He cancelled the unfavorable record of our debts. . .and did away with it completely by nailing it to the cross." (Colossians 2:13-14 T.E.V.)

"There is no condemnation now for those who live in union with Christ Jesus. For the law of the Spirit which brings us life in union with Jesus Christ sets me free from the law of sin and death." (Romans 8:1-2 T.E.V.)

Father, your love for me is hard to comprehend. Thank you for bearing with me when I'm unbearable even to myself. Sometimes I want to weep and other times just shout "Alleluia" when I catch glimpses of your forgiveness. It's so beyond the call of duty, so unlike anything I deserve. Thank you for giving me another chance, and another, and another. Amen.

FLYING THE UNITED WAY

It's hard to find God alone. True, we regularly need moments apart for God wants to make love to us in private. There He has our undivided attention. We are relatively free from outside distractions and interruptions. When we are alone, however, there is difficulty in always being sure that what we perceive to be a truth or a word from God is in fact just that. This is why God has created a community we call the Church.

I remember listening to a physics professor at a Young Life meeting in Portland, Oregon. discuss the value of the Christian community. His approach was by example. He raised the question, "What makes a good teacher?" Each of the persons present had something to share. One said, "A love for students." Another replied, "They must be motivated and interested in the subject matter." A third responded, "They need to be willing to learn from their students." The professor pressed the group, "How do you become a good teacher?" The answers came. "By attending the university and taking various courses." "By practice teaching." "By listening to and learning from other teachers." The professor made his point.

God has created a training school for persons interested in knowing and serving Him. Here they can study, share ideas, pray, receive assurance when they fail, and brainstorm how to be more effective witnesses as believers. One name given this helping community is the "ekklesia" or the Church. God is everywhere but He has promised to help us understand His presence more clearly as we gather together and regularly share with His people. The Church acts as a corrective. Our brothers and sisters keep us honest by speaking the truth in love.

In some of my classes with older youth I've asked, "What keeps the Church going?" Typical answers are, "The pastor," "money," "faithful members," "the deacons or parish council." Not once has someone ever said, "God." Maybe that's part of the problem in many congregations. We feel everything depends upon us. We need to generate programs, raise funds, win new members, recruit teachers. etc. This may be why frequently the people most concerned about serving God can be the most harried and overworked. In Scripture we are told the Church is God's idea. The Holy Spirit creates this community by inviting persons to become part of God's family through the proclamation of the Word and Sacraments. The Spirit nourishes, sustains, and empowers us so that we might in turn be the embodiment of God's love to others. As Jesus arose bodily for us, He desires to live bodily in us, and work bodily through us.

God's work is too vast for any of us to do single handed. A thumb's usefulness is greatly reduced without the fingers. It can still function but ball up your fingers into a clenched fist and now try picking up a glass of water with your thumb and the knuckle of your index finger. Frustrating, isn't it? God has created a body to do His work. The Church is more of an organism than an institution. Jesus is the Head of the Body and His Spirit coordinates and directs the movements of the Body. You can't have the Head without the Body and no one needs the Body if they have nothing to do with the Head.

The Spirit gives each member of the Body a different gift for the good of the Body. Part of our ministry to one another as God's people is to help one another discover his or her gift, that particular way they can make God's family life more meaningful and begin to realize their own potential as a child of God. Do you know your gift or gifts? The Spirit equips every believer for ministry. Just because the majority are not ordained doesn't mean they are second class citizens. All the gifts of the Body are not embodied in the clergy. Each of us has a function to fulfill in strengthening family life and building up that part of the Body where we find ourselves. As one of my friends remarked, "Not all of us are milers. Some are sprinters, high jumpers, or vaulters."

You can be religious alone but you can't be a Christian alone. Faith is personal but it's also a family affair. Christianity is knowing God in community in and through Jesus. To be a religious floater unwilling to make a commitment to some part of the Christian community is simply to affirm either one has not understood the Gospel or has not yet accepted Christ. Until we get serious with Jesus, we can be cool toward His family.

One of the ideas I'm presently exploring with several regional leaders in my own denomination is the establishment of a people bank. Different congregations could feed the names of people with certain gifts or abilities in such areas as marriage enrichment, Bible study, creative worship, goal setting, ministry to the elderly, etc. into a central location. Here they would be catalogued and then publicized. Since no single congregation is sufficient unto itself various congregations could utilize, on a short term basis, persons whose gifts they needed. This could free the clergy from trying to do everything and surface a lot of talent that frequently ends up being confined to a single congregation. I suspect that those who became involved in such an interparish ministry would be stimulated by the cross fertilization of sharing with various parts of the Body.

Each part of the one Universal Christian Church has certain traditions and practices which can enrich the whole Christian church. Each part of the one Church or family of God has certain traditions and practices which enrich the whole family. I appreciate the different flavors each group can add to the stew of God's people. In a time when many Christians are discovering each other as brothers and sisters, and all the common ground we have in Jesus Christ, I hope we don't discard the special qualities our own part of the Church can add or we'll end up being a bland gray mush. I like onions, tomatoes, and green peas.

"It is through Christ that all of us, Jews and Gentiles, are able to come in the one Spirit into the presence of the Father. You are now fellow citizens with God's people, and members of the family of God. You, too, are built upon the foundation laid by the apostles and prophets, the cornerstone being Jesus Himself. In union with Him you, too, are being built together with all the others into a house where God lives through His Spirit." (Ephesians 2:18-20, 22 T.E.V.)

"We who are strong in the faith ought to help the weak to carry their burdens in order to build them up in the faith." (Romans 15:1-2 T.E.V.)

"For where two or three come together in my Name, I am there with them." (Matthew 18:20 T.E.V.)

Father, thank you for gathering people who are not like-minded or from similar backgrounds and bringing them together to form your family. Open my eyes to the possibilities of working with my brothers and sisters instead of on my own. Help me grow in Christ and aid others in becoming aware of their gifts and the ways these can be cultivated and used. Please let me find a small group of your people with whom I can give and receive, bear and be borne. Amen.

TRAINING MANUAL FOR
THE PEOPLE OF GOD

Mark Twain is reported to have said, "What bothers me about the Bible is not what I fail to understand but what is all too clear." The Bible is read a lot but it also is misread. Satan quoted or actually misquoted passages of Scripture to Jesus during His temptation. Many persons begin reading the Bible only to get bogged down in passages where they lose their way, encounter seemingly contradictory accounts, or become confused because they hear various Christians offering different interpretations of the same passage. Then whom do you believe? How can you know whether you're interpreting a passage in a way that doesn't violate the text? After all, isn't one of the reasons there are so many different divisions in Christianity because each group interprets the Bible in their own way or to fit their particular bias?

The written word is somewhat like a tornado which hurls various objects in many directions. Different persons are hit by different truths when they read or hear the Scriptures. One person may hardly be scratched by it while another may have his entire life changed. The value and importance of Scripture is not nullified if different people hear a different message at the same time. What comforts one may upset the other.

The Bible is a story of God's dealings with His people and their reflection upon and interpretation of those encounters.

It is the witness of both individuals and a faith community. Therefore, it needs to be read alone as well as studied with others. The Scriptures record how God calls people to be His people and experience the new life He brings. But, they are more than just history. They are also a unique means whereby God exposes Himself and gathers us into a community of believers today. He speaks to us through the written Word today.

The Bible is a library of sixty-six or seventy-two books, depending on which version you use. A public library contains various kinds of printed materials and so do the Scriptures. There's poetry, folk songs, historical narrative, fables, wisdom sayings, apocalyptic literature, etc. They should not all be read in the same way for the literary style and intent of the authors differ. We can avoid a lot of unnecessary problems by searching through commentaries, concordances, and the critical introduction and footnotes of some translations for the background, literary form, and intention of the original authors.

Since the Bible was originally someone else's mail, it is helpful to know who originally wrote a letter, whom he wrote to, why, and what he said about his subject. If we take the time to dig this out we are less likely to misread or misinterpret how the Word applies to our lives and world.

Matthew's readers were Jewish so he quotes the Old Testament repeatedly to document his claim that Jesus is the Messiah. *Revelation* is loaded with symbolism because it's a persecution document written in what we would call a code so the early Christians could understand it while their Roman persecutors would think it all nonsense. It provides a tremendous statement of hope to all generations, but we do it an injustice when we try to read into it contemporary world events, or use it to predict the future. Jonah is a radical fable aimed at prejudiced people who think that God loves some groups but not others. This story deals a sledgehammer blow to racists who would exclude the minorities in their generation. When the psalmist wrote "the sun races across the heavens like a bride running to meet her groom," he was speaking as a poet. He is conveying a truth and creating a mood just like an announcer of a football game. The descriptions aren't intended to be taken literally.

Not all Scripture has the same value. It is helpful to distinguish between what biblical scholars call "revelation" and "inspiration." Revelation is the truth God discloses about Himself and His will for our lives. Inspiration is the author's particular way of conveying that truth. Thus, in the Genesis creation stories the revelation is that God made everything perfect and it all fit together. Humankind represented by Adam and Eve are designated for unique relationship with God and to image God to all creation. Therefore, humans are in a position of tremendous privilege and responsibility. Adam and Eve represent humankind. When they disturb God's ecology and choose to become their own god, they lose their lives. The three story view of the universe, the primeval garden, the talking snake, and sweet sour fruit are all means the author employs to convey this amazing truth in story form.

You may wonder, "How can I know what a particular passage means when I'm not a Bible scholar? If I can't read it just the way it's written then will I always be unsure?" Our faith does not rest in the Scripture but in Him who is Lord of Scripture. We need to be open to the unexpected as we meditate and study the Scriptures. If we approach the Scriptures slowly and persist the way we begin to study a new language, or learn a new skill, eventually we will achieve satisfying results.

Humans always seems to go from one extreme to the other. On the one hand there are those who over simplify

Scripture; and on the other those who through modern biblical scholarship are so aware of the humanness of the Scriptures, or the bubbles in the mirror and the way the silver adheres or fails to adhere to the glass, that they never see themselves in the mirror. I can't tell you how to read Scriptures, but the discipline of regular exposure pays off. Some days I may read and read and find nothing particularly new or exciting and even fall asleep over the pages. On other days I may end up underlining every other sentence.

I have found the following techniques useful:

- Read it daily, during a lunch break, while you wait in the car, to pick up a child from school, or just before bedtime. Keeping in touch with the Lord daily will deepen your relationship with Him.

- Read prayerfully. Ask the Holy Spirit to illuminate your mind and give you understanding.

- Read expectantly. If you anticipate God speaking to you and you are awake and alert you will find He does. If you approach the Bible dully it will probably be dull.

- Read with a pencil. Mark up your Bible. Note key words, subjects that interest you, passages you want to learn. Some people use colored felt pens: blue for God's promises, green for eternal life, red for the Holy Spirit, orange for our responsibilities as God's people.

- Read it with others. The Bible is the Church's book. God speaks to us when we share our insights with one another.

- Read it thoughtfully. Try and get a feel for the entire book and then read it by chapters. This will help you to place passages in context. You may find it helpful to ask the following questions: Who is writing? Whom are they writing to? Why are they writing? What are they saying about their subject? Is it true? What difference does it make to you and our world?

I drive a European car and need to rely on a good mechanic to keep the engine in tune. One morning I drove it to a local garage to have a "miss" corrected. My regular mechanic was busy. The young man who worked on my car pretended to know what he was doing. After repeated failures and road tests to correct the problem he called my regular mechanic over for assistance. The two of them were unable to solve the problem themselves. My regular mechanic finally exclaimed, "I guess we will have to go to the manual to get the 'specs' on how this type of carburator is supposed to work." It struck me that here were two competent mechanics who needed to consult a performance and maintenance manual. The Bible is a unique and contemporary training manual in which we can learn God's plan for our life, how to lay a foundation, and then begin to build for His glory. Imagine a carpenter building a house without consulting the designer's blueprint. Exploring the Scriptures alone and with other believers is essential to our life as individuals and the people of God. We need to listen to what the entire Christian community hears and then work to sift the wheat from the chaff. Yes, reading the Scripture is adult stuff and it can be a hassle, but it pays off. Don't quit plowing the field just because you strike stones.

"And you remember that ever since you were a child you have known the Holy Scriptures which are able to give you wisdom that leads to salvation through faith in Christ Jesus. For all Scripture is inspired by God and is useful for teaching the truth, rebuking error, correcting faults, and giving instruction for right living so that the man who serves God may be qualified and equipped to do every kind of good work." (2 Timothy 3:15-17 T.E.V.)

"Blessed is the man. . .whose delight is in the law of the Lord, and on His law he meditates day and night." (Psalm 1:1-2 R.S.V.).

"Above all else remember this: No one can explain, by himself, a prophecy of Scriptures. For no prophetic message ever came just from the will of man, but men carried along by the Holy Spirit as they spoke the message that came from God." (2 Peter 1:20-21 T.E.V.)

"Jesus did many other mighty works in His disciples' presence which are not written down in this book. These have been written that you may believe that Jesus is the Messiah, the Son of God, and that through this faith you may have life in His Name." (John 20:30-31 T.E.V.)

Lord, as I read the Bible, help me to be alert to your Spirit so that I may learn new truths about what you have done and are doing. Prod me that I may act out what I learn by applying these truths to my own life and sharing them with others. Give me the courage not to gloss over or ignore what bothers me or doesn't fit my understanding of you in your love letters to us. Amen.

WONDER BREAD

Without the proper nourishment the mind becomes dull, the body soft, and our resistence to disease and illness fade. Without proper nourishment the Body of Christ of which every Christian is a member becomes ineffective and lifeless. One of the ways that God has chosen to nourish His Body is through His supper.

In one of the congregations I pastored there had been a history of receiving the Lord's Supper very infrequently. When we raised the question of offering the Lord's Supper more frequently, more than one person's response was, "Won't this make it less special and more commonplace if we go to communion too often?" A young woman who had recently reaffirmed her faith stood up and said, "If you love someone can you ever get enough of Him?" That's the perspective with which the biblical witness speaks of the Lord's Supper. Coming to this meal involves meeting and receiving our Lord and not "taking it."

When I was in my teens I can remember a commercial on television for Wonder Bread. The company's slogan was their product built up your body in eight different ways. I'm not sure that coming to the Lords' Supper enriches the members of His Body in that many ways, but the Bible speaks of different reasons for sharing in this meal.

Love that is genuine must express itself. One way for two persons to communicate is by mail. A more personal form of communication is by calling on the telephone. More intimate still is a personal visit and embracing a loved one. When we come to the altar Jesus says to us what He said to the disciples, "Take eat this bread; it is my body which was given for you." When we drink from the cup He says, "This is my blood which seals God's covenant, and which is poured out for many for the forgiveness of sins." Thus, in the Lord's Supper the Lord visits us and gives Himself to us in an extremely personal way.

To say "body and blood" implied for Jesus' first disciples "Here, I am giving you my entire self." This is why the apostle Paul warns the Corinthian congregation to not take lightly the Lord's Supper for anyone who does is guilty of desecrating the body and blood of the Lord. (1 Corinthian 11:27) To simply go through the motions by rote would be like engaging in sexual intercourse casually. Christ gives Himself to us in His meal for our forgiveness and new life. It's a special sign of His love and acceptance of us. Not only do we remember His historical sacrifice of Himself for us on the cross, He remembers us and continues to strengthen us by giving us His body.

I always enjoy looking at the outstretched hands receiving the bread or host. Some are smooth and manicured, others are calloused or chapped, others are embedded with grease or gnarled from arthritis. Each of us comes as an individual. We are all different. But in making Himself one with us as individuals He also makes us one with each other. He is drawing us closer together as the members of His body. It's a wonderful thing to know that although we are all different we can be one in Him. Coming to holy communion builds community. That is why this meal is not a denominational meal but one in which all who accept Jesus as divine Lord and Saviour should be able to commune with each other.

The Sacrament is also a family thanksgiving dinner that has a present and a future dimension. In the early Christian community Jesus post resurrection meal time appearances were a fulfillment of His promise to do this with them after His death. Consequently, the mood was one of joy and celebration over the presence of the risen Lord. Within the primary worship service of the faith community each week this meal became a victory dinner in which the believers celebrated with their living Lord, His win over sin and death. Imagine a football team celebrating the victory of the critical game of the season and you have some idea of the mood that should prevail at this dinner.

The Lord's Supper was also shared in anticipation of the great Messianic banquet in heaven when all the people of God would gather together for "the wedding feast of the Lamb" to celebrate the consumation of Jesus with His bride the Church. Every time we gather and share with Him and one another in this meal there should be a sense of expectancy over ultimately doing this with Him face to face.

You may have heard someone say if a certain person doesn't want to worship that's his business. Nonsense. Who prepares supper for their family and remains indifferent if some of their children don't show up when supper is ready to be served? The Lord wants all His family to be together for supper. If someone you know doesn't show up, God may be nudging you to go and tell them the table is set for them. Happy are those who are invited to His supper and accept the invitation.

I once heard a theologian define a Christian as an ordinary looking person who gathered once a week with other people from various walks of life for a meal around a table we call an altar to celebrate the presence of an invisible host. When we share in this meal we do say something about our Lord and our faith. Proclamation is involved. But mystery surrounds this meal. We can never explain it completely.

A nine-year-old girl on her first communion capsulized it for me when I asked her what her first communion was like. She said, "Well, Jesus was there and He was loving everybody. It was great!" Coming involves acknowledging the presence of a Person and not just intellectual knowledge. So I continue to come with other hungry people and sometimes when I feel the least like being there I experience the joy of meeting the One who calls Himself the Bread of Life.

"The cup of blessing for which we give thanks to God: do we not share in the blood of Christ when we drink from this cup? And the bread which we break: do we not share in the body of Christ when we eat this bread? Because there is the one bread, all of us though many are one body; for we all share the same loaf." (I Corinthians 10:16-17 T.E.V.)

"I tell you the truth: if you do not eat the flesh of the Son of Man and drink His blood you will have no life in yourselves. Whoever eats my flesh and drinks my blood has eternal life, and I will raise him to life on the last day. For my flesh is the real food, my blood is the real drink. Whoever eats my flesh and drinks my blood lives in me and I live in him. . .Many of His disciples heard this and said, 'This teaching is too hard. Who can listen to this?'" (John 6:53-56, 60 T.E.V.)

"So He went in to stay with them. He sat at table with them, took the bread, and said the blessing; then He broke the bread and gave it to them. Their eyes were opened and they recognized Him; but He disappeared from their sight. . .they found the eleven disciples, with the others and said, 'The Lord is risen indeed! He has appeared to Simon!' The two then explained to them what had happened on the road, and how they had recognized the Lord when He broke the bread." (Luke 24:29-31, 33-35 T.E.V.)

Father, thank you for providing us with daily bread and Wonder Bread. As you have fed us, enable us to tell other beggars where they can find the Bread of Life. Help me to show my thanks by sharing my bread with the hungry of your world who have so little. Amen.

THE ELEVENTH COMMANDMENT

Do you love yourself? That may sound like a conceited question to ask but I raise it in all seriousness. Well, do you? No wavering; just yes or no. If you're not sure, then you have an exciting future as this truth strikes your life.

Jesus said, "Love your neighbor as yourself." We have heard the first part but not the second. Help the poor. Visit the sick and imprisoned. Adopt orphans. Become foster parents or foster grandparents. Buy canned goods for the neighborhood foodbank. Donate wool clothing and blankets for church relief programs. Give money for cancer research. Work for quality education in the inner city or against discrimination in housing in the suburbs. But love yourself? No way. We work ourselves to death. If we aren't involved in drumming up support for some community crisis or ferreting out political corruption, we race off to the lake or mountains, the country or ocean to get away from it all. We may come back to our jobs to rest from recreation that is often "wreck-reation."

In the dining hall of a retreat center I attended was a picture of a scrawny, knock-kneed, cross-eyed, straggly haired little girl with a smile on her face. At the bottom of the banner the artist had painted, "God makes me so glad I happened." The same idea hit me in the home of a friend who previously had a lot of negative feelings about herself. The sign on the kitchen cupboard said, "God don't make no junk."

You and I count. We have worth because God's creation is good. He loves us just the way we are — greedy and generous, honest and deceptive, patient and picky, concerned and indifferent. There is no chasm between God and us in Jesus Christ. When we know we are loved by Him we can respect ourselves. With His help we can also begin to see others as beautiful. Bald is beautiful. Black is beautiful. Almond eyes are beautiful. Gray hair is beautiful. Middle age is beautiful.

One of our daughters is in the note-writing stage. Nearly everyone who visits our home gets a note or a picture she has drawn. She gave me one that I will always treasure. It simply said, "God put luv in me so I could luv you." The apostle Paul wrote that the body of every believer is a temple of the Holy Spirit. He is present within us. When we depreciate ourselves we put Him down. When we open up to Him we can begin to know ourself and explore what we are becoming.

To love oneself does not mean we always must like what we do. Rather, self-love implies enlightened self interest, or doing what is good for oneself. It doesn't mean self indulgence. If we love ourselves we will take care of ourselves physically, emotionally, and spiritually. We can take time for personal renewal and self enrichment and not feel guilty.

Sometimes I feel like I am my own worst enemy. Nobody pushes me quite the way I push myself. Each of us can give too much, do too much for others — even for our own families — and not take enough time for ourselves. A humorless, over-scheduled, over-tired person is a poor advertisement for the Lord. Bags under the eyes, a bulge in the middle, or an uptight disposition hardly speak well of God's power to transform. If we live in Christ and He lives in us, and we daily affirm we belong to Him then we will take more time to dream and follow through on our dreams.

I asked a group of couples to rate in order of priority the amount of time and energy spent on four different roles each of them assume. They were parent — father or mother; partner — husband or wife; person — self development and care; and profession — career or homemaking. None of them put person as most important. I realize this can be over played, but it does point out a deficiency.

Do you love yourself? The eleventh commandment is, "Thou shalt not knock thyself." Another translation is, "Thou shalt not put thyself down." As long as you do, you dishonor God and rob others of what you are and what you are becoming.

"This is what love is: It is not that we have loved God but He has loved us and sent His Son to be the means by which our sins are forgiven. This is how we are sure we live in God and God lives in us: He has given us His Spirit. And we have seen and tell others that the Father sent His Son to be the Saviour of the world. Whoever declares that Jesus is the Son of God, God lives in Him, and He lives in God, and we ourselves believe and know the love which God has for us." (I John 4:10, 13-16 T.E.V.)

"When anyone is joined to Christ he is a new being: The old is gone, the new has come. All this is done by God. . ." (II Corintians 5:17-18 T.E.V.)

Thank you, Lord, for making me all that I am. Help me to be open to all I am becoming. Amen.

HOW DO YOU KNOW IF GOD IS GUIDING YOU OR YOU'RE JUST FOOLING YOURSELF?

That's a tough question. I'm always uncomfortable around people who tell me God directed them to do this, say that, or go there. Maybe I'm resentful because His answers to me aren't as intelligible. I'm not always sure what God wants me to do in a particular situation. I'm not sure if it's just because I'm especially obstinate, lack the faith, or already have my mind made up as to the desired outcome. Many times we are forced to choose or make decisions between shades of gray rather than black or white. I've seen too many Spirit-filled people pray "Thy will be done" and then agonize over exactly what course of action God wanted them to take. knowing they had to choose among several options.

It's been my experience that God is concerned with the details of our lives. I believe He can and does guide us in such matters as whether to change jobs, move to a new community, sell the house, attend a particular university, or marry a certain person. His Spirit illuminates the situation and our lives so that we can become an answer or source of help to another person wrestling with some decision. He also guides us in doing His will in our own kitchen, classroom, office, or shop. We are called to glorify Him each day. He knows how we can best accomplish that.

In seeking His will, we can do a lot of rationalizing and end up answering our own prayers. Periodically, something will be resolved in our family after considerable struggle or effort on my part. During that period I will pray for God's guidance. Once the crisis is past or the obstacle overcome, I have said to my wife, "God really helped us out in that situation." She has replied, "Who are you kidding! That was Gary Grafwallner and not God. You were so determined to have that happen how could it have gone any other way?" Sound familiar? Have you ever wondered whether in a particular instance you answered your own prayer instead of letting God? I know that I have. Sometimes we move ahead without waiting for His answer. On the other hand, sometimes doing nothing can be a cop-out too.

Faith involves trusting that God does guide us, not only in the way of salvation but our daily lives. Hind sight is always 100%. Sometimes when I'm unsure about a particular course of action I say, "God, stop me if this is contrary to your will." Or, "Make me so uncomfortable I take a different course of action." He may do just that. Once we have prayed we need to believe we will receive an answer and then listen for it. He will guide us for He wants us to know and accomplish His will. In my own life it is often "after the fact" that I experience the inner assurance that a particular happening was the answer to my prayer.

God answers prayer but He answers us in different ways. One of my friends was telling me about a conversation he had with a new Christian who was contemplating changing careers. Don asked him how he would know if God wanted him to make this move since he obviously wanted to glorify the Lord in all things. he replied, "If all the pins line up I'll move." The Quakers speak of open or closed doors which describe the same phenomena. If God wants us to do something I'm confident the doors will open, the walls will fall, things will click, and we'll be able to move ahead although it may not be rapidly but on a "proceed with caution" basis.

God can guide us through other people who may or may not be Christian. It's wonderful to be able to pray with a fellow Christian about some perplexing problem or weighty decision facing us. The answer may come while praying together, or in a subsequent conversation with our Christian brother, or when we're alone. The answer may also come through an unbeliever who cares about us and who is truthful about how he sees our situation, personal resources, and the obstacles.

God also speaks to us through the Scriptures. Within them He has placed many of His promises in writing. As we take the time to read regularly we can discover anew or for perhaps the first time His promises to us as His people. If we feel a particular course of action is not consistent with Scriptures then it's usually wise to not move against what God appears to be saying through His Word. Beware, however, of simply taking one verse out of context as a proof text answer without using a concordance to check out what the Word says in other parts of Scripture on this subject.

The Hebrews saw the Word of God, "dabar," as not simply spoken or written but action and event. The "Word of God" was any way He chose to make Himself known or communicate His will. This means that God may speak to us through a movie, billboard, pop song, tragedy, camping trip, you name it. My best cross checks as to whether or not the message I'm receiving is from God are still the Scriptures, the Christian Church, and sanctified common sense. If my stomach tells me this is not the way to go, or when I weigh all the positive elements against the negative and I end up in the minus column, God may be saying, "Use the mind I gave you."

Every believer can experience God's guidance. I'm sure I miss a lot of the signals because I move prematurely or fail to listen attentively. But faith is like learning to live with someone in a marriage. It takes a while to get to know one another, but if we spend enough time together the communication improves.

"Take delight in the Lord, and He will give you the desires of your heart." (Psalm 37:4 R.S.V.)

"Keep on working, with fear and trembling to complete your salvation, for God is always at work with you to make you willing and able to obey His purpose." (Philippians 2:12-13 T.E.V.)

"For we know in all things God works for good with those who love Him; those who He has called according to His purpose." (Romans 8:23 T.E.V.)

Father, thank you for your Spirit and the inner assurance He brings that you go before and follow after us. Forgive us when we doubt your presence and guidance. If we are open to your will for our lives, you have given us the promise you will glorify yourself through us. Help us by faith to believe this and live in the confidence we do not walk alone. Amen.

EVERY BIRD MUST WHISTLE THROUGH ITS OWN BEAK

I find a great deal of relaxation and reading in my favorite easy chair in the backyard, trudging through a field, or hiking on a high mountain trail. Often I hear the chatter of a wren, the warble of a meadow lark, the bright morning song of a robin, or the squawk of a rooster pheasant. All of them let you know they're alive by their sounds. But what's significant for me is that each bird must whistle through its own beak.

During the period our family lived in Missoula, Montana, one year went by with almost no birds around. Even the pesty little English Sparrow was scarce. It was deathly quiet. At first no one missed the birds and their songs. Soon people were asking questions and wondering about the missing birds. A large part of the problem was pollution and pesticides. Today they are coming back. Wouldn't it be a strange kind of world with no birds to praise the Lord with their songs? Wouldn't it also be a strange kind of world if the people of God were silent and the forces that could destroy life on earth were not checked?

One morning as I was studying in my office a young high school girl walked in. Her eyes sparkled and she was effervescent. I asked her to be seated and then inquired what was happening in her life. She smiled and said, "You mean you can't tell what's new?" I studied her to see if she has lost weight, gotten contact lenses, or bought a new dress. Finally I confessed I didn't know. She waved her finger and then showed me the diamond ring. "I'm engaged," she replied and then began to tell me all about her fiance. She was in love and she showed it. If we are in love with God it should show but often it may not be obvious. We can make it plain in some concrete ways.

Impression must lead to expression or it results in depression. When we begin to become aware of God's love for us, it's an unwritten law that if we fail to share what we are experiencing and learning with others we will lose it. Unless we act on what we know we cannot grow. We will stagnate. It is my observation that witnessing is one of the real poverty areas in the lives of most believers.

Witnessing has become a dirty word. In the minds of many Christians it is associated with either lots of God talk or a religious hard sell. Since most church members don't know the Scriptures well enough to teach someone God's plan of salvation, or they're afraid of being told to go to hell or mind their own business, or they are worried about being asked a question they can't answer, they end up saying nothing. Others hedge by saying, "I will let my life be a witness."

With all the visiting I do I have found that there are five dimensions to witnessing. Normally, these occur in the order I have listed them. If you do some of these but not all of them, it's like stopping in the middle of a song.

First, you must be available to people. In other words, you must spend time with them, listen to them, let them share their dreams, fears, and goals. Share your own and you'll build bridges. Normally people don't open up to strangers. All of us need friends we can trust. This is probably the most critical stage and is often abbreviated by the enthusiastic believer with subsequent sad results.

Second, meet them at their point of need. Service with no strings attached is the key here. This may involve giving them a "jumper start" on their car, taking the children so a tired mother can rest, helping them erect a fence, letting them tell you a family problem in confidence, going with them house hunting, or using your contacts to help them find a job. We are called to be servants by our Lord. All of this will help them to get to know you better and vice versa.

Third, pray for them, their families, their needs. Ask God to use you as a friend. When you talk to them pray with the back of your mind as specific concerns come up in the conversation.

Fourth, share the Gospel. This is where most people feel they must begin but that's like asking someone how his love life is with his marriage partner. If a person begins to raise "God talk" kinds of questions to you very early in your relationship then she is ready for you to proceed. Otherwise, wait until you have worked through stages one through three.

In this fourth stage be personal. Always ask them if they mind if you share your faith. Make sure they understand what you have said by repeating it. People are more interested in why you pray, the difference Christ makes in your life, why you worship, than what the Methodist Church teaches, or why some Christians emphasize baptism by immersion rather than sprinkling, or what your pastor said. Beware of answering questions they're not raising. You may want to leave a portion of the New Testament or literature.

Fifth, follow up the conversation soon and ask them to make some kind of a decision to grow. You learn to ask a closing question which leads to commitment by asking too soon and too often. This may be: to begin praying, reading the Gospel of John, attending a Bible study, beginning to worship, being baptized, becoming a member of a congregation. If people keep putting us off it simply says we haven't convinced them or they aren't buying. We need to keep in touch. A good salesman gives a customer five chances to say no. Ask them if they have reached a decision. It may mean letting them figuratively close the door in our face if that's where they are in their spiritual growth. Part of our job is planting seeds. Giant elms don't grow over night. The Lord has promised that if we are faithful there will be results from our labor.

We are born to reproduce. God wills to draw people to Himself through us. When someone does respond, it's exciting to see and share this new life with them. If you are an introvert you can witness to introverts, a businessman to other businessmen, a homemaker to other homemakers, brilliant to other intellectuals. Be yourself. Be faithful. Whistle through your own beak and you'll begin to find that others will join you in singing a chorus and living a life that praises the Lord. Telling our faith story by what we say and who we are is another window through which God discloses Himself to our world.

"But have reverence for Christ in your hearts, and make Him your Lord. Be ready at all times to answer anyone who asks you to explain the hope you have in you. But do it with gentleness and respect." (I Peter 3:15 T.E.V.)

"I tell you: whoever declares publicly that he belongs to me, the Son of Man will do the same before the angels of God; but whoever denies publicly that he belongs to me the Son of Man will also deny him before the angels of God. . .do not be worried about how you will defend yourself or what you will say. For the Holy Spirit will teach you at that time what you should say." (Luke 12:8-9, 11-12 T.E.V.)

"But you will be filled with power when the Holy Spirit comes on you, and you will be witnesses for me in Jerusalem, in all Judea, Samaria, and to the ends of the earth." (Acts 1:8 T.E.V.)

Father, open me up to the people around me who are crying for you although their need may be undefined. Forgive me for the opportunities and the lives that may be lost because of my timidity, procrastination, or repeating the lie that I don't know enough about you myself. Not knowing how people will receive us as your spokesman is scary. Give me the confidence to at least try and not limit whose life you can touch through me. Thank you for calling me to raise the dead instead of burying them. Amen.

TRAIL BLAZING

A new-found faith or a revitalized one is like falling in love. A life question for many of us, however, is, "What happens after the honeymoon?" Too many believers are like shooting stars. They burn brightly for a short while and then they disappear from sight. Maybe you have been on fire for the Lord but for various reasons that flame began to flicker and then eventually grew weaker and weaker. Or you may have watched as a person who was just beginning to bloom and grow stopped; and the buds that were about to open turned brown and fell off.

Two geologists took me on a traverse in a remote mountainous region to take soil samples for the U. S. Forest Service. Their concern was the feasibility of roads into certain areas for logging and other uses of the forest. The first day out it was sunny, the view spectacular, and flora bloomed everywhere. We camped overnight at an alpine lake. When we awoke the next morning everything was covered with snow. We were socked in with low clouds. After breakfast we separated to cover more ground in our survey. We agreed to meet back at the base camp by dusk.

One of the geologists and I hiked cross country. It was windy, wet, and cold. We made our way along the ridge tops plotting our course with a compass and contour elevation maps. Our bodies began to ache from fatigue as we pushed to reach camp on time. The day grew dark and the visibility was poor because of the bad weather. We dropped down into a valley where we were supposed to pick up an old packer's trail used by guides who brought in elk hunters during the fall. Once on the valley floor we crawled and picked our way through undergrowth for several hours. There was no trail in sight and we waded streams criss-crossing the valley floor vainly searching for one. My guide was embarassed, uptight, and dog tired.

When he was about ready to give up we spied a "blaze" or axe slash on a tree. Slogging through sand and water and driving ourselves forward we saw another slash and then a third. We had found the trail. Looking back we realized what had happened. Because the winter snow had been unusually heavy the spring run off had re-shaped the entire valley floor, washing out the trail. The only sign we were heading in the right direction was a slash on a tree above the waterline. Someone had traveled this route before. With spirits uplifted we followed the slash marks down the drainage until we reached familiar territory and then our base camp.

A plan is important when you decide to follow Jesus. There will be times that are difficult and discouraging. Unexpected situations and obstacles will come along. Without a route and a plan to follow, you may become lost or overwhelmed. What is your plan for growing in your faith? Have you set goals so you can grow in your devotional life, in studying the Bible, in your financial commitment, as a member of God's family, in your own family, and in your witness to others? Without a destination we end up spinning our wheels and wasting precious time. The Christian life doesn't just happen. God has a plan. We need to plan. Having a plan is one key to maturing in our relationship with the Lord. Other essentials are a willingness to take risks, evaluating our progress, letting others commission us, and being accountable to them.

As the people of God we can be settlers or pioneers. We can stay close to home where it is safe, familiar, and boring, or we can slowly but deliberately step out in faith to explore this life God gives us. Trusting God can be scary, but it's wonderfully exciting to see Him come through on His promises. To play it safe is to risk losing much on the brink of discovering new dimensions of His power and love.

I know of a businessman who decided to give 1/10 of his income for God's work as a result of his decision to let Christ become the center of his life. The first year he ended up borrowing money from a bank to pay his taxes. Today he has a stronger faith and is the happier for it. I know of another man in his fifties who decided to phase out of the construction business and start teaching carpentry in a trades school. His income is less but he has become a leader in improving the apprentice program in the state. This move has opened up all sorts of new opportunities for sharing his knowledge with others. I know a young woman who was intimidated by her mother and overly dependent on a confused and insecure husband. Through the encouragement of a couple of her church members she called her mother's bluff and challenged her husband to be more responsible and thoughtful. The mother has a new respect for her daughter and this woman and her husband have really begun to become one in the Lord. The apostle Paul summed it up when he wrote, ". . .in all these things we are more than conquerers through Jesus who loved us." (Romans 8:37 R.S.V.) We can know this confidence only as we become vulnerable and take risks.

Another ingredient is evaluating our progress. I remember once hearing a woman pray, "Lord, I know I'm not where I could be, but thank God I'm not where I used to be." Maybe you got side tracked and lost God in the shuffle. You may have become lazy and kept putting Him off. Maybe you bit off more than you could chew. Perhaps you tried to do too much too soon and you became discouraged or just ran out of gas.

I find it helpful to take a personal and spiritual inventory periodically. Did I accomplish what I planned to do with my family or on my job this month? Will I be able to complete it within a two week extension or by the end of next month? Am I aware of God's presence? Am I continuing to expand my horizons as a person? How am I dealing with obstacles to God's claim on my life or personal development?

I have three half-read books that are "cold" in a briefcase and a half finished cedar fence in our backyard. No one is aware of the books and very few people see our back fence, but I have unfinished business. For me, acknowledging this and completing what I started is more healthy than ignoring the facts. I think all of us live with a lot of partially completed projects and delude ourselves with the thought we are really doing a lot of things. God enables us to be honest about where we are. Sure, it hurts, but the pain is healthy.

A Methodist layman once said to me, "Gary, one of the biggest problems in church is we have no accountability. People get by with all sorts of slipshod behavior in the church and it's hurting us." I think it also hurts the individual. One way to overcome this is make yourself accountable to another Christian. Tell her what you want to do, why, and when you hope to accomplish it. Ask her to pray for you, consult with you on your progress and problems, and prod you. I find I'm much more likely to follow through on ideas and projects when Christ commissions me to do a particular work through a brother or sister. They help keep me honest. Whom are you spiritually accountable to? What for? If you never share your dreams or tell anyone where you're going, you may stop dreaming or end up spending your entire life walking around the same block over and over again.

"Behold I have set before you an open door which no one is able to shut; I know that you have but little power. . ." (Revelation 3:8 R.S.V.)

"Keep busy always in your work for the Lord, since you know that nothing you do in the Lord's service is ever without value." (I Corinthians 15:58 T.E.V.)

"And let us consider how to stir one another up to love and good works." (Hebrews 10:24 R.S.V.)

"I have the strength to face all conditions by the power that Christ gives me." (Philippians 4:13 T.E.V.)

"As for us, we have this large crowd of witnesses around us. . .Let us keep our eyes fixed on Jesus on whom our faith depends from beginning to end." (Hebrews 12:1-2 T.E.V.)

O Holy Spirit, help me to overcome my fear of the unknown. Let me claim the kingdom of this world for Christ. Give me the confidence to ask, "Why not?" when others ask, "Why?" Stretch me for your glory. Amen.

I'LL PRAY FOR YOUR RECOVERY ONLY IF YOU ONLY HAVE A COLD

Whenever God's people lose sight of one of His gifts, He always manages to make someone aware we have dropped a golden nugget into the mud. Healing is one such gift. In the last few years there has been a renewed emphasis on healing with the laying on of hands, prayers, and in some cases annointing. This has been especially true in the Charismatic Renewal Movement.

Many Christians, especially in the mainline denominations, feel rather uncomfortable about the whole business. You may have attended a healing service in some Pentacostal congregation where there was conspicuous emotionalism and been turned off. Some of us may know of persons who went forward to be healed in whom the cancer was arrested while in others it progressed. I have watched friends die an excruciating death. So why pray for healing if it doesn't make any difference? Others live in the agony of having been told, "If you only have enough faith all things are possible." But they still can't walk and they search their past and being for a reason why. What makes the waters even muddier are those instances where people do improve for no known medical reason.

I used to play it safe and say today the Lord works through physicians, nurses, and medical research to relieve pain and temporarily prolong life. God walked the earth in Jesus healing the sick. Cornea transplants, heart pacemakers, and colbalt treatments were unknown then. These are some of the means whereby God works today to bring relief and a new lease on life. One evening when we were discussing this, a friend took issue with me and jokingly remarked, "In other words, I'll pray for your recovery, Gary, if you have a cold, but not leukemia, Lou Gehrig's disease, or multiple sclerosis." I never forgot that comment.

How do we deal with the incidents of healing in the New Testament? Surely, we can't classify all of them as psychosomatic. Do we say that this kind of healing was unique to the New Testament period — a special sign of God's presence? Today God heals primarily through physicians, surgeons, psychiatrists, and small groups. That seems rather narrow. Who's to say God can or can't do what he chooses? Healing may include many factors. I believe healing is a mystery.

I remember visiting a family whose second son was to have surgery for a malignant tumor. Their other son had died two years before this boy's hospitalization. A diagnosis was made following an exploratory probe. We talked at length just prior to the surgical attempt to remove the tumor that had been discovered. With fear and trembling I asked these young parents, "What if your son dies? Are you willing to place him in God's keeping regardless of the outcome?" They weren't sure they could stand the loss of another child at such an early age. The mother was understandably resentful. Ultimately, they did say yes of their own volition. We prayed together and the parents acknowledged the boy was God's son and they agreed to place him in God's care. Having "let go" by praying "Thy will be done," we then prayed for his healing in earnest.

The boy came through the surgery and, much to the doctor's astonishment, made an amazing recovery. In a short time he was playing baseball with his friends. The family was so happy and thankful for his progress Seven months later he died of cancer with less than a week of hospitalization.

To pray for healing is not a crowbar whereby we pry out of God what He is unwilling to give us without prodding. Nor is it a magical means whereby we stroke the divine heart and manipulate the Almighty into transcending natural laws just once. It is conversation with a loving Father who wills we know Him and have life. I need to keep the lines of communication open so that I can continue to believe all things work together for good to those who love God and whom He has called to be His people. And I need the reassurance of my friends that this is not wishful thinking.

Man is a whole being. The emotional, physical, and spiritual dimensions are so interrelated that when one area is disturbed the rest of our being reflects it sooner or later. I have seen people choose to die through addiction, resignation, or grief. It's frightening. Sometimes the prayers and loving concern of friends have made a difference and sometimes it hasn't changed things one bit for the one prayed for. We can never really be sure what effect our prayers will have on any person we remember before God. I will continue to pray for those who are ill. Sickness is an enemy. It, along with all the other forces of darkness, needs to be resisted. I can't quite believe that God only wants us to pray for recovery from a common cold.

"Is there anyone who is sick? He should call the church elders who will pray for him and rub oil on him in the Name of the Lord. This prayer made in faith will heal the sick man; the Lord will restore him to health and the sins he has committed will be forgiven." (James 5:14-15 T.E.V.)

"There is in Jerusalem, by the Sheep Gate, a pool with five porches; in the Hebrew language it is called Bethzatha. A large crowd of sick people were lying on the porches. . .A man was sick who had been there for thirty-eight years. Jesus saw him lying there and knew that the man had been sick for a long time; so He said to him, 'Do you want to get well?' The sick man answered, 'Sir, I don't have anyone here to put me in the pool when the water is stirred up; while I'm trying to get in someone gets there first.' Jesus said to him, 'Get up, pick up your mat and walk.' Immediately the man got well; he picked up his mat and walked." (John 5:2-3, 5-9 T.E.V.)

Lord. I feel like I'm on thin ice with the whole subject of healing. I know I have been healed in some ways, but I'm also continually in need of healing. When we're out of touch with you, all sorts of strange things can happen to our bodies and minds. Thank you for calling yourself a physician who comes to help those who are sick. Heal me and use me to minister to all who are ill around me. When I see those whose suffering is intense or prolonged, remind me to share and be the Good News that Son suffered all sorts of pain for us and then left us a promise that the day would come when there would be no more suffering, sorrow, or death. Amen.

CAN THE BUDDHISTS BE SAVED?

Invariably, the question comes up in study groups and conversations that if Jesus is the way to the Father and no one comes to the Father except through Him, where does that leave the Buddhists. Moslems, the animists and all those who die before they ever hear of Christ? Are they lost and condemned to spend an eternity apart from God? Can you be saved and have eternal life apart from Jesus? It is written, "Salvation is to be found through Jesus alone, for there is no one else in all the world, whose name God has given to men, by whom we can be saved." (Acts 4:12) Are all these other religions just different routes to the same God?

In the Scriptures God tells us He is a God of justice and holiness. He has made us for Himself, but all of us have chosen to serve ourselves. The consequence of this is "death" or separation from God. the source of life. Each of us is held accountable. We are not all judged on the same basis, but according to how we respond to what we do know of Him. He has not left Himself without a witness in creation, history, and other people.

Those to whom much has been shown, much is required. If we know more about Him, more is expected of us. Therefore, the Inca who worshipped the sun, the Black Muslim who kneels facing Mecca, the contemplative student of Zen, and the servant of Kirshna who bathes in the Ghanges will not all be judged on the same basis as those who have learned to know of God in Jesus. The Scriptures underscore how we respond to what we perceive the will of God to be is of critical importance. Our faith is directly related to and manifests itself in how we treat other people.

Something that I have come to appreciate more and more is the common thread of truth in so many of the religious traditions of various modern and ancient cultures. People were not completely in the dark or unenlightened prior to Jesus.

The Lord desires everyone turn from their sins and be saved. He is a God of mercy and kindness because He wants every person to believe and trust Him. Salvation or eternal life is a gift of God. This life doesn't depend on what we do. While all are saved by God's gracious action toward us, not everyone has an opportunity of perceiving that grace in Jesus before they die.

In several New Testament passages the authors state that Christ went and preached to the dead of all the previous generations who were not on earth when God became a man in Jesus. Some evidently believed, and responded to His love, for it says He led a host of captives on high or out of the world of the dead. Everything we learn of God in Jesus indicates the possibility of forgiveness for all people although all do not want it.

There are enough passages in the Scriptures to safely say that all who believe in God will be saved if they freely admit they cannot save themselves. Salvation is His gift and not a matter of our efforts. I believe there are people who will be saved who have never heard of Jesus, unless today Jesus still visits the dead before the end of the age. However, at the end of this age, everyone in the entire universe will learn that through Jesus God decided to bring the whole universe back to Himself. His physical death is the way we are reconciled to God. Then every knee will bend and every tongue will confess that Christ is Lord.

Our responsibility is to prayerfully listen to each person and let him tell us what he knows of God. We cannot listen seriously to any person speaking about God unless we are open to being converted. The truth has been revealed to us, but we do not know it all. Just because someone has never worshipped Christ as God, read the Bible, or grown up in a home where the parents were Christians doesn't mean they are ignorant of God and God's ways. Sometimes they may be serving God and not even know. It's our responsibility to tell them where we see or hear God in their lives. As we have an opportunity we can introduce them to Jesus using all the intensity and passion of love language. But there must be no coercion in our witness.

Now and then I hear of someone's neighbors down the street who don't worship or openly profess to believe in God, but who are more honest, kind, and forgiving than a lot of church members. Belonging to a congregation does not guarantee you know the Lord. God is at work in the world and in the lives of many people who may be only dimly aware of His presence. We are called to discover Him and expose Him.

"Ever since God created the world. His invisible qualities, both His eternal power and His divine nature have been clearly seen. Men can perceive them in the things God made. So they have no excuse at all." (Romans 1:20 T.E.V.)

"The Gentiles do not have the Law of Moses: they sin and are lost apart from the Law. The Jews have the Law; they sin and are judged by the Law. For it is not by hearing the Law that men are put right with God but by doing what the Law commands. The Gentiles do not have the Law, but whenever of their own free will they do what the Law commands, they are a law to themselves. Their conduct shows that what the Law commands is written on their hearts. Their consciences show that this is true, since their thoughts sometimes accuse them and sometimes defend them." (Romans 2:12-14 T.E.V.)

"How happy is the servant if his master finds him doing this when he comes home. The servant who knows what his master wants him to do, but does not get himself ready and do what his master wants will be punished with a heavy whipping; but the servant who does not know what his master wants, and does something for which he deserves a whipping will be punished with a light whipping. The man to whom much is given, of him much is required." (Luke 12:43, 47-48 T.E.V.)

"When the Son of Man comes as King. . .all the earth's people will be gathered before Him. Then He will divide them into two groups just as a shepherd separates sheep from goats.. . Then the King will say to the people on His right: 'You who are blessed by my Father: Come! Come and receive the kingdom which has been prepared for you. . .I was hungry and you fed me, thirsty and you gave me a drink; I was a stranger and you received me in your homes, naked and you clothed me, in prison and you visited me. The righteous will answer Him: 'When, Lord, did we ever see you? The King will answer back, '. . .whenever you did this for one of the least of my brethren you did it for me.'" (Matthew 25:31-32, 34-37, 40 T.E.V.)

God in this age of religious pluralism I believe you are at work in different parts of the world in different ways, calling persons to yourself and then bidding them to love one another. I can't accept the idea that it makes no difference what you believe in as long as you believe in something. Help me not to hold back as I share with others what you mean to me. But then, even as I am passionately faithful to you, help me not to insist everyone become like me. Amen.

HAVE YOU PLANNED YOUR OWN FUNERAL YET?

"**H**ave you planned your own funeral yet?" I asked a ninth grade class of mine to raise this question to their parents for a homework assignment. The feedback I got was quite interesting. One mother replied, "Don't be impudent," and sent her son to his room. Another replied, "You can't be serious." While a father responded, "Hell, no, I'm only 38." None of them had a plan, although several had purchased a cemetery plot and grave marker. Most of them seemed reluctant to discuss their own death.

About the same time, I wrote each of our own parents a cover letter and a copy of my and my wife's funeral service. The shock waves came back through the mail. "We are almost twice as old as you are and we haven't done this yet. Why are you so concerned when you're so young?" Part of the reason was because I was traveling a lot in my work. The second reason was because I had been to some pretty depressing funerals where people clung to the remains in the casket, canned music from a cassette recorder was piped over the P.A. system, a paid soloist whom no one knew sang songs that were sentimental slush. And the people who had gathered couldn't wait to get out of the mortuary and change the subject to something more pleasant.

My first celebration of the resurrection at the death of a Christian was in a worship service for a young man who was deacon in my congregation. He and his wife were both very committed Christians. The whole mood of the liturgy was one of hope and joy. It proclaimed Jesus' victory over death, and the assurance that we, too, shall overcome. We sang "I Know My Redeemer Lives," "For All The Saints," and "My Hope Is Built On Nothing Less Than Jesus Blood and Righteousness." Anyone who says singing is inappropriate on such an occasion just hasn't tried it. It lifts the spirit. The Scripture lessons spoke to the brevity of human life and the unending life God offers us through His Son. We left the sanctuary to the "Hallelujah Chorus" from Handel's "Messiah" played on a pipe organ with all the stops pulled out. Unless you were deaf, dumb, and blind, you had to notice the difference. We laughed and cried and the tears were a combination of sorrow over the loss of a friend and joy over the great things God has in store for those who love Him.

The burial service for a Christian is in two parts: the worship service and the committal of the body at the cemetery. Recently I have begun to suggest to people that we have the committal portion first. That way we leave the mortuary and go in a procession to the cemetery for the graveside portion of the service. We do not end gathered around the casket, hearing the words "earth to earth. ashes to ashes, and dust to dust" knowing as soon as we leave the remains will be lowered into that yawning hole. Rather, we return to the sanctuary for a worship service of prayer, praise, and proclamation ending on a note of hope. The bereaved are surrounded by Christian friends who want to offer their support. Sometimes there is a light lunch for family and friends served in the parish hall following this. The response has been so much more positive than to the traditional funeral. After all, the service is for the living.

Death, even when it is expected, is a shock, leaving us aching, numb, confused, and upset. It is not the time to plan for one's burial. Often, we are not thinking clearly. We may be angry, disillusioned, or depressed. God calls us to live responsibly, and we should let our last rites be a testimony to our faith and the difference the Lord makes in the present and in the future.

In terms of my own death, I have chosen songs for the congregation to sing, favorite Scripture lessons, and organ music. I have requested there be no flowers and that money normally spent for this be given for World Missions. Initially, I requested a welfare casket covered by a cloth pall. Under the sign of the Cross we are all equal. Why spend money for something no one will ever see again. I have since changed my mind and have chosen to have my remains cremated. The Lord promises us a new body and this is by far the most economical way to go. A green burial is a more recent option. Your body parts could be donated to individuals or a medical school.

Some of your may want to sign a statement that permits your organs, eyes, etc. to be donated to another person. Making a legal will is another way for us to see that our loved ones are cared for and that the spread of the Gospel be continued through the Church.

Have you prepared your own funeral yet? Your funeral is too important to let someone else plan the details. Why not begin planning yours this week so that all who come can celebrate the resurrection and glorify the Lord in your death as well as during your earthly life?

"Brothers, we want you to know the truth about those who have died, so that you will not be sad as those who have no hope. We believe that Jesus died and rose again; so we believe that God will bring with Jesus those who have died believing in Him. Those who have died believing in Christ will rise to life first; then we who are living at that time will be gathered up along with them in the clouds to meet the Lord." (I Thessalonians 4:13-14, 16-17 T.E.V.)

"Let us give thanks to the God and Father of our Lord Jesus Christ. Because of His great mercy, He gave us new life by raising Jesus Christ from the dead. This fills us with a living hope. We look forward to possess the rich blessings that God keeps for His people. . .where they cannot decay, or spoil or fade away." (I Peter 1:3-4 T.E.V.)

"Jesus said to her, 'I am the resurrection and the life. Whoever believes in me will live even though he dies, and whoever believes in me will never die. Do you believe this?'" (John 11:24-25 T.E.V.)

God, I'm glad I don't have to be afraid to die. I know in part but still have a lot of questions about death. I am glad that Jesus resurrection frees us from the power and finality of death. Help me to share the good news with those who are still afraid to come to grips with their own physical death so they can begin to live before they die. Amen.

THE OTHER SIDE OF THE GRAVE

D o you ever find yourself wondering, "What will it be like when. I die? Will I see God? How will I be different? Will my family ties remain or be broken? Will my body change? Will I be recognizable? How does reincarnation fit with the Christian belief in resurrection?"

I believe we cannot live confidently in the present unless we know that the future God planned for us is better than our earth life.

I make it a habit to call on persons who visit our congregation. In one such home I learned that the wife had a terminal illness which brought about a spiritual and emotional crisis during the past year. As we talked I shared some Scripture passages that dealt with life after death. She got very upset and insisted she didn't want to hear about it for fear it would shake her faith. In effect she said, "This is destroying my idea of the hereafter. I can't bear to have you tell me it's not the way I pictured it. So please leave me alone."

If that's where you are, perhaps you shouldn't read what follows. Since the early Christians who wrote the New Testament believed the return or second coming of Jesus was right around the corner, they didn't write a great deal about the period between His ascension and His return. As Christians died, the Church was forced to come to grips with the condition of those who died before Jesus' return. Much of what was written is suggestive and not as specific as a great deal of the writings of various religions. The fact that writers are so economical in their description of life after death suggests they were almost afraid to say too much for fear of misrepresenting God and misleading His people. That's one of the reasons I'm leery of people who seem to have all of the answers about the hereafter.

One truth declared repeatedly is that life is found in our relationship with God through Jesus Christ. Eternal life is knowing the Father and Jesus. If you believe in Jesus you have eternal life. Because of baptism, we are told we no longer live but Christ lives in us. "He who has the Son has life; whoever does not have the Son of God does not have life." To have eternal life means that a person is in a right relationship with the Lord. This relation is not terminated by a cessation of bodily functions.

When a believer dies, his relationship with God continues but he does not go to heaven. We are told the relationship is more intimate than on earth but not face to face. That is reserved for heaven the end of this age. Jesus said to the thief who repented, "Today you will be with me in Paradise." He doesn't say, "Today you will be with me in heaven."

Many biblical scholars feel that "Paradise" is the New Testament equivalent for "Sheol" or the place of the dead in the Old Testament. Paul in his letter to the Philippians in jail writes, "For me to live is Christ; if I die I will gain more." The implication is one of greater intimacy. Perhaps we'll be more aware of His presence. No where does Paul say we will see the Lord face to face at the moment of death.

The author of Revelation describes the condition of the saints who have experienced martyrdom because they have proclaimed Jesus Lord as being "under the altar." When they cry for vindication they are told "to rest a little longer." The Church is not yet joined in marriage to Jesus the Lamb. In the story of Lazarus and the rich man, following their deaths Lazarus is carried to "the bosom of Abraham" and the insensitive rich man finds himself in Hades. The former is not, however, spoken of as being in heaven, nor the latter in hell. Elsewhere Christians who die in the Lord are spoken of as "asleep" in Jesus.

In summary, a believer's relationship with the Lord is deepened following death. We are more than the flesh and bones that decay in a grave or tissues that are consumed in a crematorium following death. While we are temporarily separated from our loved ones, nothing separates us from God's love toward us in Jesus.

Heaven and hell are biblical realities and are experienced at the end of the age. Hell is the exclusion by our own choice from God's presence forever and ever. It is irreversible and mighty uncomfortable. Far from being a place of physical torment, the real crunch comes in that we are cut off from the God who is life. Hell is the most severe form of death. Darkness, gnashing of teeth, wailing, a closed door, the fiery lake all are descriptions of the woeful realization you could be with the Lord but that forever and ever you will be separated from Him.

The growing body of knowledge concerning the mind has disclosed mental anguish can be more severe than any physical pain. I picture hell as a setting where nothing is together, everything is half hearted, incomplete, unfulfilled. Everyone does just what he wants to do. No one helps his neighbor. You get what you can while you can. Forgiveness is forgotten. The end justifies the means. Love in any form is not permitted.

Heaven will be experienced as a reality when God's kingdom comes in all its fullness. It may be on the earth but it will involve more than just the earth. There "will be a new heaven and new earth;" another way of saying all of creation will be renewed.

Heaven is also referred to as a new Eden. It will all fit together as God Intended in the beginning. There will be a perfect spiritual ecological balance. As Isaiah described it, "The wolf will live with the lamb. . ., the cow and the bear will graze and their young will lie down together. . .and the lion will eat straw like an ox; and the nursing child will play by the hole of the cobra." In other words, each part of the creation will be in harmony with the others. There will be no more suffering, sickness, war, or death.

The people of God from every nation, generation, and ethnic background will be gathered together to enjoy and serve the Lord and one another. The famous and the unknown saints will join in a visible fellowship. God will be the obvious and essential center of all activity. There will be all sorts of possibilities to explore and discover. In our earth life we function far below our potential. I like to think then we will be running on all eight cylinders or maybe twelve or sixteen, instead of four cylinders. We will know Him as He now knows us. It will be beautiful beyond words. Is it any wonder John described it as like a jeweled city sparkling with the presence of her creator? The blind man will see. The deaf will hear the sound of music and the words "I love you." The crippled will have new legs. We will be given an incorruptible body.

To say I believe in the resurrection of the body is to say I believe that I will always be. Modern physics has taught us you can't destroy matter but you can change its form. We will receive a new casing but all that makes you "you" as an identifiable and unique person will not be lost. It will be intensified and purified.

Humans will always be human, never less than man or more than woman, as the belief of reincarnation teaches. Previous family relationships such as husband and wife and parents and children will be transcended because Jesus said marriage is for the earth only. All who have done the will of the Father will be together as brothers and sisters and relatives in the same family. Imagine what it will be like to celebrate a birthday or a special occasion in such company. There will be no loneliness or fear, only peace, joy, music, and laughter. Obviously, I'm excited!

One morning as I was going to work an older man asked, as a courtesy, how I was doing. I told him I was glad to be all right, he replied, "Well, when you consider the alternative I feel the same way." I answered, "Oh, I plan on being around forever." He looked at me as if to say, "It's a nice trick if you can manage it. Who do you think you are — God?" "No, but I am one of His sons," I said, God's promise is that all who believe in Him as Saviour and Lord shall live forever. Our bodies go through a physical transformation but we do not die. I don't understand it. I celebrate the fact that because He lives we shall live, too, forever and ever.

"To have faith is to be sure of the things we hope for, to be certain of the things we cannot see." (Hebrews 11:1 T.E.V.)

"We, however, are citizens of heaven, and we eagerly await for our Saviour to come from heaven, the Lord Jesus Christ. He will change our weak mortal bodies and make them like His glorious body, using that power by which He is able to bring all things under His rule." (Philippians 3:20-21 T.E.V.)

"For we know that when this tent we live in—our earthly body here on earth—is torn down, God will have a house in heaven for us to live in, a home He Himself made, which will last forever. We know that as long as we are at home in this body, we are away from the Lord's home." (II Corinthians 5:1,6 T.E.V.)

"Jesus told them, 'Believe in God, believe also in me. There are many rooms in my Father's house, and I am going to prepare a place for you. I would not tell you this if it were not so. And after I go and prepare a place for you, I will come again and take you to myself, so that you will be where I am.'" (John 14:1-3 T.E.V.)

Father, it sounds too good to be true. I believe, help my unbelief. Alleluia. Amen.

THE BEGINNING

The Apostles' Creed

I believe in God, the Father almighty, creator of heaven and earth.

I believe in Jesus Christ, God's only Son, our Lord, who was conceived by the Holy Spirit, born of the virgin Mary, suffered under Pontius Pilate, was crucified, died, and was buried; he descended to the dead:

On the third day he rose again; he ascended into heaven, he is seated at the right hand of the Father, and he will come to judge the living and the dead.

I believe in the Holy Spirit, the holy catholic church, the communion of saints, the forgiveness of sins, the resurrection of the body, and the life everlasting. Amen.

The Nicene Creed

We believe in one God, the Father, the Almighty, Maker of heaven and earth, of all that is seen and unseen.

We believe in one Lord Jesus Christ, the only Son of God, eternally begotten of the Father; God from God, Light from Light, true God from true God; begotten not made, one in being with the Father. Through Him all things were made. For us men and for our salvation He came down from heaven. By the power of the Holy Spirit He was born of the Virgin Mary and became man. For our sake He was crucified under Pontius Pilate. He suffered, died, and was buried. On the third day He rose again, in fulfillment of the Scriptures. He ascended into heaven and is seated at the right hand of the Father. He will come again in glory to judge the living and the dead, and His kingdom will have no end.

We believe in the Holy Spirit, the Lord, the Giver of life, who proceeds from the Father and the Son. With the Father and the Son He is worshipped and glorified. He has spoken through the prophets. We believe in one, holy, catholic, and apostolic Church. We acknowledge one baptism for the forgiveness of sins. We look for the resurrection of the dead and the life of the world to come. Amen.